A Strang

THE LIFE
OF ANNA KAVAN

ALSO BY JEREMY REED AND PUBLISHED BY PETER OWEN

Angels, Divas and Blacklisted Heroes

Bitter Blue: Tranquillizers, Creativity, Breakdown

Boy Caesar

Chasing Black Rainbows: A Novel Based on the Life of Artaud

Delirium: An Interpretation of Arthur Rimbaud

Diamond Nebula

Dorian: A Sequel to The Picture of Dorian Gray

Inhabiting Shadows

Isidore: A Fictional Re-creation of the Life of Lautréamont

Lipstick, Sex and Poetry

Madness – The Price of Poetry

Red Hot Lipstick

When the Whip Comes Down: A Novel About de Sade

A STRANGER ON EARTH

THE LIFE AND WORK
OF ANNA KAVAN

Jeremy Reed

PETER OWEN
LONDON AND CHESTER SPRINGS

PETER OWEN PUBLISHERS

73 Kenway Road
London SW5 0RE

Peter Owen books are distributed
in the USA by
Dufour Editions Inc.,
Chester Springs,
PA 19425-0007

First published in Great Britain
by Peter Owen Publishers 2006

ISBN 0 7206 1241 1

A catalogue record for this book is
available from the British Library

Printed and bound in Great Britain by
Windsor Print Production Ltd, Tonbridge, Kent

For Peter Owen, Anna's publisher, and for
Lene Rasmussen and Stephen Barber

'I seem to be able to dream practically anywhere. It really seems to have been my principal occupation throughout life, which probably explains why I've had so little success in the world.'

Anna Kavan, 'The Cactus Sign'

'When I'm rushing on my run
And I feel just like Jesus' son'

Lou Reed, 'Heroin'

'When Anna would look out of a window, she could see more in a minute than most would see in a lifetime. She was extraordinarily perceptive, intuitive, visionary.'

Raymond Marriott

Acknowledgements

*

THE AUTHOR WOULD like to thank the Leverhulme Trust for a grant that made the writing of this book possible. A debt of more than gratitude is extended to Rose Knox-Peebles, whose devotion to Anna's memory, hospitality and willingness to make available her private collection of Kavan paintings and memorabilia were of invaluable assistance to the author.

My thanks go to Stephen Barber for his constant encouragement throughout the undertaking of this project and to John Robinson for a lifetime's support in sustaining my morale in writing one uncompromising book after another.

I would like to thank Peter Owen, Francis King and Bruce Hunter, all of whom gave generously of their time in recalling incidents of Anna Kavan's life.

Likewise I am indebted to Lene Rasmussen for research and photography, to James Allen at Red Snapper for giving me a preview of Anna's paintings and to Aaron Budnik for gifting me rare Kavan editions. Special thanks go to my dear friend Karl Orend for research and invaluable enthusiasm.

Thanks are also extended to my friends David Tibet, James Williamson, the late John Balance and Martin Stone, all compatriots in rehabilitating the dispossessed, and to the Hampstead Tea Rooms where most of this book was written.

My thanks, too, go to Edmund White for helping instigate the writing of this book and to Moon and Martha as prompters from the cat dimension.

I would also like to thank James and Suzanne Hallgate of Lucius Gallery for permission to reproduce paintings from their exhibition on Anna Kavan. The chapter 'Exploding into Colour' was originally published in an illustrated catalogue of Anna Kavan's paintings put out as a Lucius/Punk Daisy Publication in 2005.

Thanks also to Jenny Sturm, who is in the process of writing a dissertation on Anna Kavan's New Zealand years, for information pertaining to Ian Hamilton.

Contents

*

Illustrations between pages 112 and 113

The illustration on the inside front and back covers is based on a self-portrait in oils painted by Anna Kavan, reproduced by permission of Peter Owen.

The paintings by Anna Kavan on pages 1, 5-7, 9 and 10-16 are all reproduced by kind permission of James Hallgate.

The photographs on pages 2-4, 7, 8, 16 are from the collections of Rose Knox-Peebles, the McFarlin Library of Tulsa, Oklahoma, and Peter Owen.

Introduction

*

ANNA KAVAN, KNOWN in three previous incarnations as Helen Woods, Helen Ferguson and Helen Edmonds, did everything she could to resist biography. Continuously reinventing herself, both as a person and as a writer, she systematically destroyed all of her diaries except those covering the period between July 1926 and November 1927, as well as the majority of her correspondence and private papers. Reluctant to concede even the date of her birth, she lived and died as an enigmatic outsider, a writer whose mystique is inseparable from her reputation. One of the most imaginative of British novelists, Anna Kavan was a lifelong heroin addict who, while rarely making the drug the subject of her work, none the less operated from it as a source.

I have attempted in *A Stranger on Earth* to look at aspects of Anna Kavan's life and work, uniting the two in short chapters that link biography to her predominant characteristics as a writer. The discovery of 'The Cactus Sign', an unpublished account of her wartime travels in the years 1939–42, has provided me with a detailed chronology of events during this previously unmapped period of her life, and so, too, the recent retrieval of a large number of her paintings from a London house clearance has allowed me as an offshoot to write about her explosively visionary art.

David Callard's authoritatively investigative biography, *The Case of Anna Kavan*, provides the building blocks to an indispensable, even if sketchy, chronological sequence of Anna's life. My book looks at the person, the addict, the myth of somebody who intended to be 'a thrilling enigma for posterity' and in part at the underlying social ethos of the 1950s and 1960s, the decades in which Anna Kavan wrote her outstanding books, including the cult classic *Ice*.

Anna Kavan anticipated becoming 'the world's best-kept secret; one that would never be told'. If my interest is primarily in rehabilitating the dispossessed, then I have tried in *A Stranger on Earth* to re-create something of Anna Kavan the person as well as direct attention to a body of work that is both vitally modern and, by its originality, truly great.

1

Tasting the Blues

*

THE SPRING WAS early that year on the Côte d'Azur, the curve of the coast disappearing under a white sky, the abundant almond and cherry blossom lifting pink sleeves – and of course the privileged were there: not the fashionistas, directors and glitterati of the film festival but the rich expatriates who lived in the luxurious turreted villas or mini-castles overlooking the bay and who engaged in the leisurely pursuit known as the Promenade des Anglais. This was Cannes at the beginning of the twentieth century, with its palm trees from Africa and the Middle East, eucalyptus from Australia and bougainvillaea and yuccas from the Americas, and it was here that Anna Kavan was born Helen Emily Woods on 10 April 1901, in a house called Les Delices, in a fashionable resort favoured by the moneyed class to which her father Claude Charles Edward Woods, a landed gentleman of independent means, belonged.

Woods, whose family owned a vast estate called Holeyn Hall in Wylam, near Newcastle upon Tyne, had met and married Anna's mother, Helen Eliza Bright, when he was in his mid-thirties. Seventeen years younger than her husband, Helen Eliza Bright was distinguished by her vivacity, good looks and considerable intellect and was the granddaughter of Dr Richard Bright, who had at one time been physician to Queen Victoria. Helen Bright would seem to have passed on to her daughter a facility to reinvent her past, in that she claimed fictitiously that her father had been an Austrian count. She was in fact illegitimate and without means and in marrying Claude Woods succeeded in securing the wealth that she seems to have regarded as a priority.

In the first of a series of familial rejections Anna was sent away soon after birth in the care of a nurse called Sammy, before returning months later to live with her parents at Churchill Court in west London. The child was denied parental affection or seemingly even contact – she was allowed to visit her mother each evening for ten minutes before dinner – and thus introduced into the emotionally cold world that would adversely affect her personality for the rest of her life. Her sense of abandonment was reinforced at the age of four when her parents went to live in America, leaving her and her nurse with relatives in Pepper Street, Southwark, London. A year later her father returned and took her and Sammy to New York and from there to Rialto, California, where he had bought an orange grove.

At the age of six Anna was sent to an American boarding-school, and for the next seven years suffered an excruciating sense of betrayal, alienation and acute loneliness that went with boarding-school life. Her isolation was further magnified by the fact that she was often left in the school during holidays. Painfully, self-consciously aware of her difference from the other pupils, she retreated into a rich fantasy world of her own creation.

When Anna was fourteen her father committed suicide by jumping from the stern of a ship bound for South America. That the incident was to have a profound traumatizing effect on her life is evident in the feelings she expressed about his death in the unpublished story 'The Mists':

> Though I'd hardly known my father, I had built a fantasy round him, believing that, when I was older, he would make me his companion and give me the affection I longed for. By dying he seemed deliberately to have destroyed this hope and condemned me to lifelong loneliness. Now I felt myself alone against the whole world, more alone than I'd ever been . . . I couldn't forgive my father for abandoning me, or my mother for her indecent haste in putting him under the ground.

Anna was now totally dependent on her mother, who reacted against the social stigma of suicide by removing her from her American boarding-school and sending her to another, this time in Lausanne, Switzerland.

Anna's already dislocated schooling was again disrupted when she was sent back to England within a year to attend a progressive girls' school – Parson Mead in Ashstead, Surrey. Anna seems to have taken a dislike to life at Parson Mead, where she claimed the headmistress made sexual overtures, and she was withdrawn by her mother and sent to Malvern Girls' College, where once again she was the exception in being forced to stay behind at school during the holidays. It was at Malvern that Anna made a friend of Ann Ledbrook, cementing a friend-ship that was to last for life. Anna was at Malvern during the First World War, but the reality of its military atrocities seems to have made no lasting impression on her, unlike the Second World War in which she was to lose her son and be a witness to a London devastated by the ferocity of the Luftwaffe's nightly air raids.

Despite a ruptured, loveless childhood characterized by discontinuous edu-cation, a father's suicide and the manipulative hostility of a socially scheming and overbearingly egotistical mother, Anna was sufficiently advanced academi-cally to be offered a place at Oxford. She returned from Malvern College to her mother's new home at Manor House, Earley, but despite receiving from her an annuity of £600 on her eighteenth birthday Anna allowed her mother to dis-suade her from accepting the place on offer at Oxford.

Helen Bright, who had struck it rich by marrying at eighteen, was deter-mined that her daughter should do the same. Although Anna had travelled widely in the course of a peripatetic childhood and been educated in America and Europe as well as a variety of English schools, the sheltered nature of her upbringing that entirely excluded male contact, together with her naturally shy and introspective character, had left her relatively inexperienced and with little knowledge of the adult world. Taking advantage of Anna's immaturity, her mother attempted to decide her future by introducing her to Donald Ferguson, who was rumoured to be one of her own ex-lovers.

Pursued by the lasciviously scheming Donald Ferguson – who at thirty was twelve years Anna's senior and who falsely laid claim to descending from a Scottish branch of the aristocracy – Anna was undoubtedly flattered by the attentions of an older man and by the prospect of life in Burma, where Ferguson was employed as an engineer on the railways. Pressurized by her mother and doubt-less anxious to escape the suffocating domestic climate at Earley, Anna agreed to marry Donald Ferguson and in so doing effectively surrendered her indepen-dence. It was a decision that was to have disastrous consequences for her still formative character, both psychologically and sexually, and led in time to the extreme reaction against social convention that forms the subject of this book.

2

An Enigma Called Helen

*

IN THE TWENTY-FIVE years in which she lived under the alias of Anna Kavan, she expressed little or no interest in the six novels she had published between 1929 and 1937 under her married name Helen Ferguson. None of the books was reprinted in her lifetime, and like most writers Kavan probably felt embarrassed by a style she had superseded and a subject matter from which she had grown radically disconnected. In the course of a lifetime artists continually reinvent themselves, and from the 1940s onwards Anna Kavan had no room in her life for Helen Ferguson.

We know little of the person Helen Ferguson other than the biographical facts of her marriage and the information contained in her diaries covering the period July 1926 to November 1927. What we do have, though, is a detailed account of her short-lived and explosive marriage to Donald Ferguson filtered through her obsessive reworking of the subject in various forms in her fiction. *Let Me Alone* (1930) is a directly autobiographical re-creation of Helen Ferguson's school days and marriage, aspects of which recur in the story of the fictional 'Anna Kavan' in *A Stranger Still* (1935) and are revisited in the compulsively hypnotic *Who Are You?* (1963), Anna's final attempt to liberate herself from the excoriating traumas of a marriage fuelled by alcohol on one side and drug addiction on the other.

The haste with which the match had been made suggests that her mother's choice of Donald Ferguson was opportunistic, almost random. He had little or nothing in common with the introverted, sexually inexperienced teenager, and the disdain Helen soon came to feel for him, both physically and mentally, is clear from her fictional portraits of the marriage.

The pair were married at St Peter's Church, Earley, on 10 September 1920. In *Let Me Alone*, the third novel published under the name of Helen Ferguson,

Anna's proto-feminist, yet unfailingly romantic, sentiments are clear.

> She felt both astounded and indignant, as though he had in some unexpected
> way made her ridiculous. She had never even thought of marriage. She didn't in
> the least want to marry anybody. She wanted to go through life alone, in her own
> independent, detached fashion. The idea of being bound up with another per-
> son in such a relationship as marriage was hateful to her. And then, to marry a
> person like Matthew Kavan! Her very heart shuddered.

Acutely disappointed at being denied the chance of an academic career,
Helen reluctantly followed her husband out east to Burma. They travelled via
Ceylon to Rangoon by steamer and from there to Mandalay and his house, The
Chestnuts. She unforgettably re-created this house in the fetid, swampy atmos-
phere of her novel *Who Are You?*, where the protagonist is raped by her husband,
the violent tenor of the marriage exacerbated by the intolerable heat.

The Fergusons' social life was limited to other colonials, for social inter-
course with the Burmese was forbidden. Donald's heavy drinking and Helen's
sullen withdrawal into the world of imagination soon put an intolerable strain on
the marriage, leading to bouts of acute rage on both sides. *In Let Me Alone* Helen
Ferguson describes her fictional persona Anna as emanating 'an aura of isolation
that was like something tangible'.

There's also a strong suggestion of lesbianism in the novel, and this was perhaps integral to Helen Ferguson's sexual make-up, for Anna in *Let Me Alone* has
an affair in college with a bohemian girl called Sidney. This may in part account
for Helen's real-life resistance to her husband's sexual demands and her refusal
to give herself to him during their London honeymoon when they stayed at a
hotel in Jermyn Street. In a directly autobiographical narration of the events of
her marriage night, Anna obdurately resists her husband, driven by physical
loathing.

> The horrid part was though he stared hungrily at Anna, he did not seem to see
> her at all, as an individual. She, personally, did not exist as far as he was con-
> cerned: he had reduced her to a sort of extension of himself. He missed her out
> completely. And now his blue eyes met hers with a gleam of complacent antici-
> pation – self-congratulatory, it appeared – as if he prided himself on his rights
> over her. And he was going to exercise them, too. Oh yes, he meant to exact his

husband's pound of flesh. There was something a bit pasha-like in his attitude towards her. The age-old, man-to-woman tyrannous condescension. He began to approach her with his prancing gait. But she slammed the door in his face, shutting him out, and turned the key on him. Just as the door closed, she saw the death of his neat smile, and the ugly, spiteful look, mean and cunning and in some way almost imbecile, taking its place. She shuddered, and her heart beat quickly. But the goblin-brightness stayed on her face.

It is likely that someone as chronically phobic and introverted as Helen Ferguson would express initial fear at the demands of a man who, even if he was her husband, was none the less a stranger. Although the marriage effectively ended in 1922, having barely survived two years, the emotional damage remained for her lifetime. The residual traumas were to endlessly resurface in the fictional works of both Helen Ferguson and Anna Kavan, although both were at pains to conceal that there was a child born of the union and that Helen Ferguson returned to England with her son Bryan in 1922, as an unwelcome product of her shattered marriage.

The positive side of the extreme alienation Helen experienced in her life in Burma was that she had started writing there, presumably as a way of coping with her depressed state and excruciating vulnerability. Helen may well have argued that, on account of the rudimentary medical facilities available in Burma, it was safer to return to England with her child. Donald Ferguson, it seems, made no attempt to stop or to accompany her, suggesting that both partners accepted the breakdown of their marriage. It is clear from the tone of the Ferguson/Kavan books that a mutual and venomous hatred had replaced any attempts to even tolerate each other and that compromise was no longer an option.

He began to hate her for eluding him. He hated her because he knew that she despised him. He hated the way she had of looking coldly at him when he spoke to her, and then turning away her face in a gesture of cold, indifferent contempt. It made him feel he could kill her.

(*Let Me Alone*)

Donald Ferguson clearly lacked the imaginative facility and more feminine aspects that Helen required in a man. Without a base of her own, or a clear purpose in life, the young Helen Ferguson returned to her mother's house in Earley, and alternated periods there with regular visits to the South of France where she

was first introduced to a bohemian drug culture that had emerged as the hedonistic reaction of a new generation to the atrocities of the First World War.

There are no written records of Helen Ferguson's life covering the period
between 1922, when she returned to England after the break-up of her marriage,
and the diary entries documenting the beginnings of a new relationship in 1926.
She spent the winter of 1925/6 in the South of France, and it was there in the
village of Sainte-Maxime on the Cannes coast that she met the painter Stuart
Edmonds and fell desperately, almost dangerously in love.

Edmonds, a person of independent means, was the wealthy son of a depart-
ment-store owner from Kingston-upon-Thames. He was married, with a son,
but separated, the strictures of his family's Catholicism on moral grounds making divorce difficult. The situation was additionally complicated by the fact that
Edmonds was travelling on holiday with his mistress Phyllis Morris.

The bohemian Edmonds resembled Helen's first husband in that he, too,
appears to have been an alcoholic, only he was a leisured dilettante who painted,
unlike the rigidly conventional Donald Ferguson with his mechanical belief in a
male work ethic.

Helen's innate existential mistrust of life, together with a faculty for ruthless
self-analysis, was already beginning to shape her character, as is evident in the
first diary entry for 1926, in which she reflects on how even a modicum of happiness would go a long way towards making the present more tolerable.

> Real life is a hateful and tiresome dream . . . yet how happy I might be with just a
> little happiness. I possess in the highest degree the art of making a little bit go a
> long way, and I am not affected by what affects other people . . . I realise com-
> pletely the hopeless nature of my character. And yet, I still have a certain conceit;
> I still feel superior to the majority. This is curious. Perhaps I feel superior
> merely because I understand and analyse myself more than other people . . .

Helen succeeded in spite of Phyllis Morris in beginning an affair with Stuart
Edmonds in France, and they continued seeing each other on their return to
England. In July 1926 she moved for a time to a hotel in Bedfordshire, close to the
village of Aspley Guise where her son Bryan was being looked after by a nurse.
She continued to be so traumatized by the emotional fall-out from her failed
marriage that she visited her son only occasionally, disturbed by the fact that he
kept a photograph of his father; the associations still shook her to the core. Her

dependency on heroin was already a feature in the diary. She was by this time seriously dependent, referring to heroin as H in her diary entries, a significant pointer to the fact that the Helen Ferguson novels were, like the Anna Kavan books, all accompanied in their writing by the chemical addition of her 'clean white powder'. In a note of flattering self-appraisal, she writes: 'The H makes one's eyes beautiful. There is no doubt that I am attractive. I watched myself in the glass for a long time, which gave me real pleasure.'

There was no stability to her mood, apparent in that she attempted suicide by slashing her wrists after a violent altercation with Edmonds, before rushing herself to hospital in a taxi. She focused obsessively on Edmonds as her reason for living. For the first time her diary records what was to become both a lifetime's preoccupation and the source of her work – her fear of madness. 'I am much more abnormal; indeed, at times, I really am afraid of going mad.' Whether the disturbing symptoms she was starting to experience were induced by the drugs or the strains of the relationship isn't clear, but there were signs of a growing dissociation and a tendency to hallucinate in her account of a walk taken to overcome the need for drugs. 'This afternoon a curious thing happened to me. The reality of everything began to recede. I felt lonely and inaccessible and forgotten, and had a number of illusions, sometimes vivid and sometimes unreal. There were two sisters, one of whom talked about a river.'

The problems in Helen's relationship with Edmonds stemmed in part from the fact that his father threatened to discontinue his allowance if he lived with Helen. Helen had moved into a small flat in Chelsea and was becoming increasingly habituated. 'My ankle hurts me a lot and I took more drugs than usual . . . I have to take so much now to feel the least effect,' she noted on 3 August 1926. Edmonds objected to Helen's taking drugs, but she was expected to tolerate his abuse of alcohol.

On 18 August Edmonds's divorce was decreed absolute, and by way of celebration the couple immediately took off to the South of France. However, any chance of enjoyment was dashed by Helen's need to have an abortion. The unpleasantness of the termination and its after-effects were the only option she could contemplate, given the association of childbirth with the irreparable damage done her by Donald Ferguson. In the initial rush of her relationship with Edmonds Helen had made herself sexually available, noting with clinical detachment in her diary whether she had achieved orgasm, although she soon came to repeat the pattern established in her first marriage of demanding her own room and thus bringing an end to sexual relations with Edmonds. *The Honeysuckle Girl*, a fictional re-creation of the marriage written by her long-time friend Rhys Davies and drawn from first-hand accounts she had given him, portrays her locking the bedroom door to prevent her husband's entry and regularly rendering herself senseless with sleeping pills as a means of deferring his advances. Unlike Donald Ferguson, Edmonds seems to have accepted Helen's increasing aversion to sex and to have taken mistresses in compensation.

There was something radically missing in Helen's life at this stage, a cause of frustration apparent in her diary entry for 2 October, in which she identifies a need for dedicated work.

There is one type of happiness which I have never experienced: I mean the happiness of 'work'; the satisfaction which is to be derived from being intensely occupied and from the sense of achievement from having created something. I think that before I die I ought to try and experience that. Death is so irrevocable one ought to be very certain that there is nothing desirable left in life before killing one's self. When I was very young and trying to write I used to feel something of what I mean – a distinctive kind of contentment, very moderate and comforting and unemotional. It is a pleasure rather less precarious than most because it does not depend on any outside person or circumstance, but purely on one's self. Probably I have become incapable of experiencing it through living too much on my emotions and allowing myself to depend for happiness entirely on people and personal relationships, but I think I ought to try to make the attempt. Driving in the car this afternoon I elaborated a plan for trying to experience it. The first essential is to cut myself off as completely as possible from all my present associations. I must disappear. No one must have my address. My allowance and any necessary letters I can fetch from Cooks. I must get a room somewhere very cheaply in London: go somewhere to draw, and really work hard all, all, all the time. I could go to the Chelsea Polytechnic classes and learn to sketch as well. Whenever I am not working, I must be cooking my food or doing something of the kind – never be unoccupied for a moment. I could change my name to cut myself off more completely from the past, and be Arlen. That is too theatrical, really, but it wouldn't do any harm. I wonder if I would ever have the energy and determination to do it. Of course not unless Stuart abandons me completely. It is interesting to contemplate. Is it just my natural cowardice and the self-preservation instinct urging me away from suicide?

Helen's resolve to be independent and write surfaced in October, when she decided to break with Edmonds temporarily and take a room in London. Something of the liberation that she felt at the prospect of living alone in London, changing her name and tasting big-city freedom is reproduced in the decision taken by Beryl, in her first novel *A Charmed Circle*, who runs away from her oppressive home, the Vicarage at Hannington, and finds work and a commodious room in Knightsbridge working for a stylish female milliner. In the novel Beryl is more exhilarated than frightened at launching herself on the world and is undoubtedly articulating Helen's feelings when, having taken in the minimally furnished but bright room which is hers, she realizes with relief the consequences of what she has done. 'She went to the window and stood there, drawing in deep breaths of freedom and the cool night air. No one knew where she was. No one would control and harass her any more.'

That significant inner shifts were occurring in the 25-year-old Helen's life is clear from the way she had already prefigured her future as a solitary artist. Even at this stage she contemplated changing her name in the interest not only of dissociating from the past but of reinvention. The problem for Helen was that Stuart Edmonds demanded from her the sort of emotional support that she in return needed from a man. Her relationship with him not only exposed her vulnerability but denied her the support she had hoped to find in a more sympathetic partner. Her diary entry recording the dilemma is characteristically astute. 'I know he is not the type of person who can support or protect anyone else: he needs support and protection too much himself.'

Yet Helen was in love for the first and only time in her life. This was the reason she gave Raymond Marriott for not having destroyed her diaries relating to this period, and it was also obvious from her refusal to let go of a man who as a psychological type was undeniably the wrong choice for her.

On 5 October, with considerable trepidation, she went to visit Edmonds's father, a man who ruthlessly talked finance and not emotions. Stuart had advised her to offer £300 a year towards the upkeep of the relationship, but his father demanded £2,000 a year, which must also be used to support Stuart's son, John. He also stipulated that his son's name should not be cited as co-respondent in the divorce case Donald Ferguson would bring. Helen's allowance could not possibly stretch that far.

She was now using cocaine to compensate for a messy relationship which was also conducted in secret, to evade parental scrutiny. Her mother visited her on 12 October intending to persuade her to study art in Dresden as a way of doing something positive for herself and focusing her life. Helen's dilemma, as she began the second of the two surviving diaries, was that she felt insecure on two main counts. The prospect of attending Dresden Art School filled her with dread, and at the same time her fine-tuned faculty for self-analysis informed her of the fundamental flaw in her relationship. This time her perception appeared spot on. 'The fact is, of course, that we are too temperamentally alike, we both need to learn, but neither of us is strong enough to support the other.'

As a compromise for her mother Helen decided to attend classes at the Central School of Art under the tutelage of Bernard Meninsky, a charismatic Ukrainian who had made a reputation for himself as an inspired teacher. In her diary she expressed ambivalent feelings about her new occupation.

> The curious thing is that I think I shall like being at the Central London. It's a tremendous relief to have an occupation which exacts all one's attention . . . When I am drawing – even dreary things like casts – I do not think how nice it would be to have a friend in the room because I am not bored. The same when I am reading something that interests me or writing this diary or exploring the recesses of my mind.

Underneath it all, she was not only unhappy but acutely aware that the source of her depression was not a response to an adverse environment but was founded on a much deeper ontological basis. However, she was gradually finding a way to incorporate her negative symptoms into the positive experience of her life – her ability to write about it and evaluate her emotional reactions.

Two weeks after enrolling at the Central School of Art her diary entry for 30 October recorded her aspiration for a more optimistic and comfortable state of self-acceptance. Helen would never be normal, but her stripped-down analysis of herself is interesting for its contradictions.

> I want to live a primitive, animal sort of life, with one chosen man who satisfies me physically and with whom I can talk nonsense, behave childishly or be silent just as I please. I want to sleep a long time, eat a lot, sit about in the sun and be sexual pretty often. I don't want anybody else at all. I don't want the bother of being friends with people and having to talk to them. I don't want emotional (or any other) excitement. I want to love and be desired and appreciated. I want to

be comfortable and happy and at peace – not all strung up and excited as I am now whenever I am happy. My tastes are not in the least cultured. I dislike most plays, all reviews, picture galleries and 'highbrow' music. I prefer not to change my clothes during the day; not to eat elaborately served meals; not to wash more than is absolutely necessary. I would rather go to bed than sit up and dance. In fact I am an animal; a lazy, intelligent, unsociable animal.

Here she is projecting her own opposite, the normal person she could never be, with simple tastes, a strong sexual appetite satisfied by a monogamous partner, capable of stabilizing her moods and achieving contentment – so different from the suicidal thoughts provoked by her uncertain relationship with Edmonds.

Helen was now living in her own flat in Francis Street, Victoria, and although upset by her mother's refusal to recognize her individual needs she still looked to her for emotional support. 'If Mother weren't in town I don't think I could bear my existence,' she wrote. 'She has been most awfully kind to me, taking me out nearly every day and giving me lots of presents.' Her mother certainly knew that she was already habituated and suffering periodic memory lapses as well as renewed episodes of paranoia and dissociation.

On 14 December, now renting an apartment at Albany Mansions, Helen received a note from Donald Ferguson informing her that she would hear from his solicitors. The prospect of divorce was now immediate, and she remained suicidal despite eliciting from Edmonds a promise that even if he did not marry her he would at least live with her in London. In fact he seems to have feared commitment, and towards the end of December he took off alone on a holiday to Switzerland and stayed away for six weeks. The final diary entry on 29 January 1927 finds Helen totally despairing about her life. She is gripped by the apprehension that Edmonds will never return. 'Always before I think I've hoped in my heart for happiness even when I was most despairing, but now I've almost stopped hoping.'

As part of her desire in later life systematically to eliminate the facts of her past, Anna Kavan destroyed all the diaries she continued to keep about her troubled life and relationships. The attempt to manipulate time was a prominent characteristic of Anna's, even to the point, like Jean Genet, of never admitting to a birth date. People who live in and write directly out of their imagination are often reluctant to reveal biographical details, usually because their lives involve the need to continuously re-create reality through fiction, a process that in turn leaves them feeling inalienably remote from the concrete facts of their past. Helen Ferguson and Anna Kavan were two distinct people, and while they shared the same genes one could argue that the cellular modifications brought about by prolonged heroin use succeeded over a period of time in altering Anna Kavan biologically into her own creation.

3

Whisky, Breakdowns and
a Bulldog Named Olga

*

ELEN FERGUSON BEGAN sustained
writing soon after she and Stuart Edmonds set up home at Albany Mansions.

The relatively new star in publishing, the up-and-coming Jonathan Cape, who had a name for spotting individual and experimental writers, was enthusiastic enough about Helen's books to put out three novels in quick succession – *A Charmed Circle* in 1929 and *The Dark Sisters* and *Let Me Alone* in 1930 – investing in her talent rather than hoping for the sales that might be generated by books of distinct literary merit.

The accelerated creative pace of the late 1920s suggests that Helen gained from the stability of a permanent relationship, although there is no record of the couple ever having married, and Helen continued perversely to publish under the name of her despised first husband, perhaps as a way of insulting him for his refusal to acknowledge her identity. Although in her social life Helen owned to the identity of Helen Edmonds while she lived with Stuart, she was to continue to publish books under the name of Helen Ferguson throughout the 1930s.

In 1930 Stuart Edmonds bought a house called The Elms, in the Chiltern village of Bledlow Cross in Buckinghamshire. Helen was responsible for designing the interior décor of the house and supplemented her allowance by breeding bulldogs. It was a big white house on a hill that Anna Kavan later recalled in the novella *My Soul in China*, written after the collapse of her relationship with Edmonds.

Very tall trees grew at the back of the house, and higher up at the edge of the field there were five more elms, bending away from the south-west wind. Sometimes, especially on wet autumn afternoons when they had lost most of their leaves, these five looked like the spectres of drunken giants reeling away from the wood that fitted down snug as a moleskin cap on the brow of the hill. There was a gate at the edge of the wood where you got a good view of the house, and for a long time, for years, I used to walk up there and sit on the gate and look back at the house, and it was always the same, curled up like a friendly white animal sunning itself, or sheltering under the trees.

Although Helen seems rarely to have alluded to the fact, Stuart's refusal as a Catholic to use contraception resulted in the birth of a girl, and it was probably an enormous psychological relief to her when the child died in infancy, freeing her of the inevitable creative sacrifice that comes of being a mother. Little is known about the child, and Helen's natural tendency to suppress emotion meant that she largely buried her existence in the disinformation that substituted for her past.

What was important to her was that she was writing and winning something of a reputation for literary novels which, while they subscribe to a conventional use of plot and linear narrative, are none the less harnessed to an undertow in which the fear of madness exploding out of character is a psychological given. If Helen Ferguson's fiction differs from the books put out under the name of Anna Kavan, it is only because Helen's evolution as a novelist did not yet allow for the deconstruction of form and the liberating subject matter of drugs and madness that are so much a part of Anna Kavan's writing. Helen Ferguson submerges her life as an addict into the general psychological disquiet of her characters. The drug was in her veins, but she keeps the secret subcutaneous.

Shortly after her move to Bledlow Helen met the novelist Rhys Davies, who was to become a lifelong friend and to play a particularly supportive role in her later life. His recollection of their first meeting provides one of the few contemporary character sketches of Helen that we have. The two established an immediate mutual sympathy.

My first glimpse of her had been when she arrived with her equally personable husband at the Lechlade fishing cottage he had lent to a mutual friend and myself. She was a young woman coming over the pretty bridge spanning the young Thames where a trout stream joined it and where swans came to be fed below a window of the stone cottage ... Later I saw her gambolling in Bledlow with her cherished bulldogs, animals that always seem to me to conquer a high-strung temperament of neurosis by sheer weighty power of muscles and flesh.

She and her husband lived luxuriously in Bledlow. There were social exchanges, a country pond placidity, and the village cricket team as championed by Helen's generous husband. She painted in thick oils, wrote her well-controlled novels; she had a son by her first husband.

It all sounds too normal: the idyllic rural prospect, the couple's financial security, social engagements, uninterrupted time for Helen in which to write and paint, the additional camaraderie of her dogs; but something was wrong. After her early creative flurry Helen did not publish a novel for five years. Eventually she produced *A Stranger Still* in 1935, by far the best of the Helen Ferguson novels and the first to give voice to the more decadent aspects of modernism that were to become her milieu: cars, drugs, disaffection with convention and the profligacy of a new generation of bright young things.

Helen was by this time totally dependent on heroin. Since she had not registered with the Home Office and was thus not receiving a subsistence dose from her doctor, somewhere out in the sticks she must have had a dealer, and so she would have been subject to the brutal inconsistencies of a source that would doubtless have left her in need. That she could finance her habit we know, but her ability to network with the underworld is all part of the furtive aspect of her character that others noted in her inveterate tendency to lie. Anna kept her secrets dark and hidden as a stone in a well, and the flagrant rows that erupted between the chauvinistic Edmonds and his self-regarding partner, who appeared detached from awareness of others, must often have centred on their mutual dependencies: alcohol and the clandestine manner in which Helen got her drugs.

An additional source of frustration to Edmonds must have been their rivalry as painters. He was in fact a painter only in name, whereas Helen exhibited her paintings at the prestigious Wertheim Gallery in London in 1935.

As the relationship began to break down, Helen's obsession with self-harm resurfaced. There was at least one serious suicide attempt preceding the separation that led to her being sectioned, recorded with deliberate attention to detail in *My Soul in China*.

All at once, despair coils itself neatly inside my head, leaving no room for any other feeling. I snatch a steaming cup of tea from somewhere, and with the utmost haste I start dissolving in it tablets of veronal, tuinal, sodium amytal, etc., etc. As if I were catching a train and hadn't a second to lose I keep stirring more and more tablets into the hot tea, until the contents of the cup are solid like blancmange; this nauseous mess I cram into my mouth with a spoon.

Helen was growing to despise Edmonds's boisterous bonhomie, his drinking, his overt philandering at the local pubs and his attachment to cricket as an area in which he could to some degree show an amateur expertise. He was drunk most of the time and was letting himself go; his violent mood swings as a result of his alcohol addiction reminded her of her altogether better concealed addiction with its less manifest side-effects. The incompatibility of their temperaments was reflected in their choice of chemicals, each angered by the other's remoteness and unwillingness to communicate honestly. Each must have blamed the other's altered state for their volatile, mutually hostile relationship.

Frustrated in his ambitions as a painter, unfulfilled in his personal life, dependent on his inflexibly moralistic father for an income and denied children by Helen, Edmonds was also starting to lose his looks. With ruthless detachment Anna Kavan in the last decade of her life described his alcoholically mapped dissipation in the story 'Now and Then', published posthumously in *Julia and the Bazooka*. Telling the cold facts in the present tense, she evokes his premature burn-out with the precision of an autopsy.

Now he doesn't work at all any more. He's given up painting and all his other pursuits. Now the only thing he likes is to lie on a bed or sofa, doing absolutely nothing . . . Now he lounges about all day in a dressing-gown, untidy, unshaved. When he does dress, his expensive clothes look as if they had been passed on by someone else, too tight for him, unpressed, stained with food, drink, ash, God knows what . . . the first time I went out with him I remember he wore a blue shirt and corduroy trousers as soft and white as milk. He was very attractive then, very sexy. He wasn't exactly slim, but certainly not at all heavy, just muscular and solidly well-proportioned in the brown masculine Mediterranean way, with an aquiline profile and beautiful sea-coloured eyes set in long, long lashes. Now he's put on weight and it doesn't suit him. It makes him look middle-aged, mediocre. His skin is still brown, but somehow it looks unhealthy, more like jaundice than sun-tan. Outwardly, and in every other way, he's become totally unlike the man I married.

Edmonds's degeneration was in part accelerated by Helen's remoteness, asexuality and drug use and undoubtedly made worse by his realizing that she had played a substantial part in bringing about the changes in him that she so despised. He had previously known coldness in Helen; now he faced contempt. Neither now resembled the person the other had married. Helen injected her sense of reality, and Stuart came at her with ropy breath, the furred residue of his unremitting hangovers.

He had by now come to symbolize all that Helen most disliked in men: arrogance, cynicism, a bravura enthusiasm for sport and its spill-over into the pub. According to Raymond Marriott, Edmonds's alcoholism had reached such an advanced stage that Helen had to revive him in the mornings by holding a glass of brandy to his lips. Like so many drunks he had grown quarrelsome at home, verbally lashing out at Helen for her refusal to socialize and her abstinence from sex. It was a vicious circle. His drunkenness encouraged her to take refuge in drugs, while he blamed her habit for his immersion in drink. Helen would rush out of the house and take off for long drives across the countryside – she loved speed – to be free of his tyrannically oppressive mood.

It may have been the nervous exhaustion attendant on a turbulent domestic life that froze Helen's fictional output during the first half of the 1930s. Inherently lacking in self-esteem, and easily knocked if criticized, her creative energies were temporarily undermined by having her character continuously shredded by her truculent partner.

In the book that finally took shape out of her life with Stuart Edmonds, *A Stranger Still*, the fictional character Anna Kavan analyses Martin's unpleasant characteristics:

> This man whom she loved was so incomprehensible to her. Why, in the midst of their peaceful happiness, did he suddenly become antagonistic? She did not understand that this was how his ego asserted itself, in little spurts of uncalled-for viciousness now and again. He was inconsistently resentful in spite of his independence, and inconsistently selfish in spite of his amiability, and inconsistently vicious if anything troubled him.

The negative components in Edmonds that Helen had been only too willing to overlook in the initial stages of their relationship had become distorted by her tendency to provoke his shadow side. She was periodically visiting an analyst in

Wimpole Street, London, an episode alluded to in *My Soul in China*, where the
analyst is given the name Max. By this time she had tried on several occasions to
leave Edmonds and start an independent life, but she had always and catastrophically returned. Six years before her felicitous meeting with the psychiatrist Dr
Karl Theodor Bluth, she was already in therapy and fast developing a facility for
self-exploration that was to become a determinant of her fiction.

> The clock ticks on to the next second, traffic murmurs discreetly in this
> decorous street, and Max, enigmatic and expressionless as any Oriental, is
> suavely telling me that I ought to go back to the house where I used to live in the
> country before it's sold. 'Yes, you're quite sufficiently stabilized now; it will give
> you confidence.'

Already the Helen Ferguson novels display a profound knowledge of psychological motives won from extreme experiences, a gift that the evolving author
was to share with Anaïs Nin; both women learnt their perspicacity first hand in
the emotional arena and the complex vicissitudes of relationships.

It was at this juncture that Helen's mother, who was in England and staying
at Claridges on a visit from her new home in Constantia in South Africa, was told
of her daughter's chronic addiction in a letter from Edmonds. Mrs Woods, who
had recently conducted a marriage of convenience with a wealthy homosexual,
Hugh Tevis, decided that the best course of action was to pay for her daughter to
undergo detoxification in a London clinic. This was the first of Helen's many
attempts not to kick the drug but to modify the extent of her dependency
through narcosis. Better than complete withdrawal or involuntary withdrawal
necessitated by an irregular supply, the treatment effectively substituted chloral
for heroin. According to Rhys Davies, Helen had been misregulating her injections
and had developed abscesses on her thighs owing to a shortage of clean needles,
in part caused by her refusal to register with the Home Office as a user, which
would have given her access to clean needles and a manageable amount of the
drug. The private clinic was amenable to most of Helen's personal requests,
including her demand for smoked trout from Harrods, and its therapeutic policy
was refreshingly non-judgemental, but she remained reluctant to come off
heroin. Her nihilism and mistrust of people, together with an even stronger dislike of reality, made it hard for her to be persuaded of the advantages of being
drug-free. She was suspicious too of the tolerance shown her by the clinic.

It was as treacherous as anything else involving human beings. The shadowy depression remained like a hair shirt on her passive body. She must endure it. The place did not promise cure, only believed in it as a liberation she must achieve mainly by self-discipline, since she could not stay there for ever. Its advisers and ministers wished to prolong the gift of life. To what purpose?

(*My Soul in China*)

Mrs Woods agreed to pay for her daughter's detoxification only if she consented to see a psychiatrist on a regular basis, an arrangement she hoped would contribute towards repairing Helen's marriage. She even decided to increase Helen's allowance as an incentive to stabilize and offered to buy a number of her paintings as a further token of encouragement. She was understandably terrified, given her daughter's vulnerability, that if Helen broke with Stuart Edmonds and her rural life at Bledlow she would eventually turn up at her own home and expect to be taken in. She even advised Edmonds to compensate for Helen's lack of sexual interest by taking a mistress. She never confirmed or denied Helen's unshakeable belief that she was illegitimate, but she was adamant that she was not going to take responsibility for Helen on the rebound from her second marriage. She dreaded the mess that Helen would get into if she was left to her own resources and much preferred that her daughter keep up the pretence of marriage. She herself was married to a man who had not the slightest interest in her sexually, but the arrangement provided her with both the convenience of wealth and congenial company. Mother and daughter seem to have shared an attraction to gay men, but Mrs Woods feared her daughter's more unconventional features, such as the drug-taking and the strange behaviour bordering on madness. Helen's drug withdrawal was only partially successful, but the experience provided her with the clinical imagery and the metaphor of a cell that became recurrent motifs in the work of Anna Kavan. Her inner landscape of addiction and fear of madness at this time paved the way for Anna's obsessive mapping of these subjects in fiction in the 1960s, when they were highly topical. Helen's fictional characters are often interestingly abnormal but never pathological in the manner of Anna's character studies. Her life had not as yet become fused with her art, and there was still a separation between author and subject necessary to the sort of novel she was writing.

Mrs Woods, who spent much of her time travelling, went on to Florida, via Morocco, leaving her daughter with the daunting prospect of resuming life with her ambitionless and estranged husband. In *My Soul in China* Anna Kavan turned the spotlight on her own disturbed state at the time, when Kay's Australian friend confronts her with her parasitism.

> You use me as a psychological prop all the time. You feed on me emotionally . . . Max called you a psychological gold-digger, and you're a parasite too. When he said what a mess you'd made of Martin I defended you and said that Martin must have been a mess to start with. But my Christ, I don't wonder now the poor bugger was finished. No one on earth could stand up to it. You'd ruin anyone's life.

There is little doubt that Helen Ferguson was a glacial, introspective user, preoccupied with her rich inner world at the expense of growing within a relationship, but that is not to say that she was incapable of loving or being loved. Almost all of the fiction written by Helen Ferguson and later by Anna Kavan has as its dominant theme the need to find love and the pain involved in the attempt. Hers is always a woman's story involving hurt, rejection and the re-creation of the two major relationships that continued all her life to drive splinters of glass into wounds that would not heal. When Rhys Davies commented that all her novels are essentially the same novel in terms of their thematic preoccupations, he was in a way right, although *Ice* is a radical exception.

Helen returned home to her favourite bulldog Olga, but her frigidity towards her husband remained fixed. She resumed painting, read *Anna Karenina* in bed, attempted writing poems that never got beyond a single stanza and relied on sleeping tablets to blank out nights spent alone in her room with the door locked.

One night she scrawled a note for Edmonds, who was out at the pub: 'I want to stay in my room tonight. Don't bring any food, shall go to bed. I want to sleep. Will take two of those sleeping tablets they gave me. Love Helen.' In fact she emptied a bottle of thirty sleeping tablets. Suspicious that he was getting no response to his repeated and urgent rapping on Helen's bedroom door, Edmonds broke in, saw the empty bottle on the bed and knew immediately what had happened. An ambulance took her to the nearby cottage hospital, her stomach was pumped and she was given a private room in which to recover.

This time Helen had gone too far, and Edmonds was unable to cope. The already overstrained marriage was now effectively at an end. Her mother was shocked into the realization that Helen was serious about wanting to end her life and packed her off to a private clinic in Zurich. She survived this suicide attempt, but symbolically she had killed off three identities: Helen Woods, the unhappy child who had hardly known her parents or received any modicum of love; Helen Ferguson, the inexperienced young woman brutally violated by an unsuitable and possessive husband and whose novels had made her a modest name; and Helen Edmonds, the junkie, mismatched to the cantankerously dipsomaniacal Stuart Edmonds. Three further novels were published in quick succession under the name Helen Ferguson in the mid-1930s, this time with John Lane as the publisher, since she had been dropped by Jonathan Cape because of low sales: *A Stranger Still* (1935), *Goose Cross* (1936) and *Rich Get Rich* (1937), the last of which disappeared without notice or trace. But a new personality emerged from the wreckage of her past, carrying the name of the fictional persona in her 1930 novel *Let Me Alone*: Anna Kavan. The brunette, elegantly and formally dressed Helen Edmonds was dispatched in the Zurich clinic, to be replaced by an emaciated, blonde, strikingly made-up woman in her late thirties with a vaguely East European name and a determination to write the sort of books that Helen Ferguson would never have dared.

4

Helen Ferguson's Novels

*

NOTHING OF HELEN Ferguson's early writings stemming from her life in Burma in the years 1920–22 has survived, but we do know from later allusions that she was writing seriously for a long time before publishing her first novel at the age of twenty-eight. Her marriage to Donald Ferguson had thrown her deeply in on herself and, lacking sympathetic company among the conventionally stuffy colonials, her only constructive dialogue was to be found in reading novels and writing. As a solitary child growing up in a series of boarding-schools she had probably always been bookish. Married to a man who blamed her for his every frustration, no matter how minor, she became too frightened to act and instead took to imagining alternative realities, rather as she later used drugs.

Her first novel, *A Charmed Circle* (1929), like its successor *The Dark Sisters* (1930), takes as its subject the contrasting lives of sisters, Olive and Beryl Deane, who are engaged in the struggle to liberate themselves from the suffocating oppression of their home, the Old Vicarage in Hannington, which is ruled over by a taciturn, almost sociopathic father who has totally submerged himself in a self-taught programme of reading.

Beryl, the younger and more adventurous of the sisters, manages on impulse to break with her home and run away to London, where she takes a live-in job as a shop assistant to a voguish milliner. It has been suggested, although without corroboration, that after Helen's first marriage broke up in 1922 she opened a small fashion boutique in Chelsea with a working partner. Certainly the familiarity with fashion, displayed to fine effect in *A Charmed Circle* and again in the fictional Anna Kavan's business enterprise in *A Stranger Still*, suggests a working knowledge of the subject. Is the description of the boutique jointly run by Anna and Catherine in the bohemian Chelsea of the early 1920s a factual re-creation of a shop designed to accommodate Helen's own lifelong enthusiasm for fashionable clothes?

For the shop was so nearly being a success. They had plenty of customers, thanks to their advertisements in the most exclusive fashion papers. The original, somewhat startling garments had caught on, particularly in certain theatrical circles. And the queer showroom in Beauchamp Place with the sombre velvet curtains, the elaborate pelmets, and the wild, rather sinister designs painted on the tall double doors was effective to say the least of it. A sort of Russian ballet effect, off stage.

In *A Charmed Circle* Beryl's employer, the capricious, partying lesbian Miss Aguilar, seeks to manipulate her psychologically and sexually before throwing her out of her life. Beryl returns to her stagnant home, having had a bite of big-city life, and becomes a rival to her depressed sister Olive's hopes of marrying Will, a young farmer.

Helen had not yet found her voice as a writer, but she proved in her first novel that she could write well. And already the obsession with madness that was to grow in Anna Kavan's novels into a singular theme is expressed in the one real relationship in the novel – the bonding of Olive and her equally morose father through their shared depressive nature. *Punch* described this as the first novel of a writer who showed considerable promise. 'Cancel the allusions to extroverts and the inhibitions and there is an eerie originality about her book's aloofness from normal and fashionably abnormal life. I feel she has found neither herself nor her milieu, though the pains she has taken to persuade me suggest she may yet make use of both.'

The reviewer was right about the book's 'eerie originality', an apt description of the trait that Anna Kavan would inherit from Helen Ferguson of writing novels in which reality intermittently dips out of focus to be replaced by a hallucinated alternative. The book was also noted as 'A powerful exposition of contained lives' by the *Times Literary Supplement*, while the *Sunday Telegraph* commented on her style, in which 'Not a word is wasted in her spare but painterly prose.'

Her second novel, *The Dark Sisters* (1930), comes out of the same substrate as her first, although it is set in the London of the 1920s, where female emancipation is a major issue. Emerald and Karen belong to a generation living through rapidly evolving social changes; they are able to manage their independence,

Emerald as a fashion model and Karen as a more reclusive dreamer, prone to retreating into a fantasy world. Karen is the object of criticism for her introspection, as Helen Ferguson had been for the remoteness that comes of living in the imagination rather than on a more accessible plane of reality. Clearly defending her own preference for subjectivity, Anna has Karen attempt to vindicate her apparent passivity by arguing it with her boyfriend Edmond.

> 'Why shouldn't I let my imagination run away with me?' she asked, in her curious drawl. 'If I prefer the dream to the reality, what does it matter? It is only I who am concerned in any case.'
>
> She laughed inwardly at the idea of his daring to question her secluded world. She did not take him seriously. But he was indignant and dispirited, without any consolation, infinitely removed from her detached contentment.
>
> 'You are not the only one concerned,' he complained bitterly. 'Do you think it is pleasant for your friends to feel that you are always miles away, thinking of something else? That they are of no importance to you?'
>
> 'I don't compel people to become my friends,' she replied, somewhat sarcastic.

As with the inconclusiveness of the ending in *A Charmed Circle*, in which Beryl and Olive are resentfully returned to the status quo, so Emerald, who has taken Karen out of London on account of her vulnerability, returns her to the city so that she can resume her imaginary life there. The action of the book is like a loop in which language itself is the experience, rather than the emotional resolution arrived at by the characters. The ambivalent reviewer for the *Times Literary Supplement*, arguing that the surface glitter of the prose deprived the book of a clear storyline, lamented 'that so much talent should be wasted on such trivial material'.

Let Me Alone (1930) is the definitive Helen Ferguson novel; it establishes a perception central to all of Anna Kavan's later fiction, of an alienated narrator living tangential to what passes as reality and increasingly terrified by the precariousness of human relationships and the fundamental isolation at the core of individual experience. Through her fictional persona Anna-Marie Forrester, Helen strips away the social niceties, the pretence of marriage and even more so the psychological compromise that comes of attempting to be normal. She also stresses the need for women to cultivate resistance. As in her own first marriage,

Anna-Marie is subjected to 'a personal, deliberate cruelty, but that more devastating cruelty that comes from indifference, from sheer, absolute, deadly carelessness, the ultimate affront'.

Although never politically affiliated, in *Let Me Alone* Helen was unintentionally anticipating the much later feminist approach to women and marriage, so much so that on the book's reissue in 1974 the reviewer for the *New Statesman* called it 'a pioneering effort for Women's Liberation', noting that Anna Kavan was viewed posthumously as 'one of the saints of Women's Lib and the drug culture'.

Some of the glacial reserve that friends who did not meet her level remarked on in Helen Ferguson's character is reflected in *Let Me Alone* in Anna-Marie's dispassionate and ruthless dissection of her husband's insignificance. The description of his redundant attributes is a clear pointer to how in her own life Helen had come to perceive the progressively deteriorating Stuart Edmonds.

> She looked at him. She looked coldly, dispassionately at him . . . Only she saw his obtuseness, his stupidity, his crudeness. He was uninteresting. He was nothing. She had got inside the parcel at last, and there was nothing there. The ultimate secret of her surprise packet revealed itself as a blank. He was nothing at all. She did not specially dislike him. But she resented having to live with him. Living with him was almost too much of an insult. Her cold, indifferent eyes watched him, and repudiated him. He would never be anything at all to her. Even though she yielded him her body.

Five years on, in *A Stranger Still* (1935), Helen is exploring less nihilistic territory, although the strained relationship between the fictional Anna Kavan and Martin Lewinson, who is clearly Stuart Edmonds, is relieved only by the sharing of a hedonistic summer interlude in the South of France, where the affair begins and ends. In its emotional intensity this novel captures something of the heady rush Helen initially experienced on first meeting Edmonds.

The realization that her life and happiness were not dependent on a man's making strongly colours Anna-Marie's actions in the racy bohemian atmosphere that pervades *A Stranger Still*. As if facing herself full-on in the mirror, Helen has the fictional Anna Kavan reflect on what it means to be an intelligent and independent woman.

The sense of unreality had left her; she felt clear-headed as never before. She stood there in absolute honesty, looking into herself. She was suddenly, objectively, aware of the girl Anna Kavan, an individual human being, alive in the world, alone, without support, without obligations, capable of intelligent thought and responsible for her own destiny.

As in *Let Me Alone*, Helen portrays her mother as a fictional aunt Lauretta, a self-regarding, idle dilettante occupied with playing bridge in the unostentatious luxury of hotels in the South of France, bored with her routine, uneventful days and worried principally about the conspicuous bulge in her figure. There is another mention of the shop in Beauchamp Place, which Lauretta subsidized, again prompting the question whether Helen had run a boutique without any aptitude for business, in the process sinking her mother's investment.

Unable to let go her legacy of pain, in *A Stranger Still* Helen reviewed the disaster site of her first marriage, like scar tissue reopened. The sad figure of Matthew Kavan, Assistant Locomotive Superintendent to the Central Shan States Railway Company, wearing a white tropical drill uniform, is of course none other than the boorish, truculent Donald Ferguson, imperiously barking orders at the natives, fried on whisky and nursing sexual fantasies about a wife who had deserted him.

There is a provocative charge of rebelliousness in this novel and a sense of connecting with a more liberated sexual ethos, as though the author is confident of the new values espoused by her generation. The book was well received, the reviewer for the *Illustrated London News* commenting: 'Helen Ferguson, whose books are always good, has done nothing better than *A Stranger Still*. She sees people very clearly: she sees women through their pretty skins and turns them inside out. *A Stranger Still* is a complete drama in which every actor is fitted out with a significant part.' The *Sunday Times* endorsed this approval: 'It lives from start to finish ... The theme of the book is the essential solitude of the individual. It engages the mind uncompromisingly, and its style is well knit.' The book was recommended by the Book Society.

In a renewed bout of creativity, Helen chased hard on the tail of her critically acclaimed novel by publishing *Goose Cross*, a mysterious fantasy novel set in a Chiltern village modelled on Bledlow Cross, the following year. The book marked a departure from her by now established menu of themes. Life in the Chilterns had clearly seeped deeply into her unconscious; *Goose Cross* aligns landscape and history with the present, making it an early precursor of psycho-geography, as well as an ethno-fantasy novel that shared affinities with John Cowper Powys in bringing the myth of place alive through imaginary re-creation of the potency of archetypal symbols.

A curse descends on Goose Cross at the end of summer and at harvest time, brought about, it is intimated, by the discovery of a Roman skeleton. In another clear parallel with her own life Helen depicts Judith Spenders fighting to save her marriage to her alcoholic husband Thomas, who is captain of the local cricket team. The couple also breed bulldogs. When the curse is eventually lifted from the village those who have survived are gifted not with revelation but at least a fuller perception of life.

The novel, more an excursion of the imagination than one of inductive plot, marked a change of tack for Helen's work, but the lack of positive response to the book seems to have warned her off continuing in this direction. Again it is the novel's fine descriptive prose, and its predominantly dark, brooding aspects that point up affinities with Anna Kavan's later, more experimental prose. In reviewing the book, the *Times Literary Supplement* singled out the qualities of imagination and rich vocabulary as her prime assets. 'In fairness to her, however, it is necessary to add that she writes with considerable force, has a powerful imagination and a wide range of language. Those readers who have a taste for the "death-dark uni-verse" will find here material to their liking.' The *London Mercury* was equally guarded in its praise, noting: 'Miss Ferguson draws on most of the literary con-ventions of the modern English country novel. Cosmic awareness, the sub-life of inanimate objects and mysterious influences of haunted pools appear intermit-tently. Nevertheless, the three dozen or so characters who she keeps on the move excite interest.'

Rich Get Rich (1937), Helen Ferguson's last novel, and the one that preceded the serious mental breakdown that so dramatically changed her life, is rooted in the Thoreau-like idealism of Swithin Chance, a man who moves through the experience of working with the mentally ill, marrying a rich woman and divorcing her, becoming a tutor, but remaining essentially without a clear purpose in life. Swithin Chance becomes attracted to Mary, the sister of an old school friend who runs a leftist bookshop, and decides to go back to nature, live self-sufficiently in a cottage and idealistically write of his experiences, almost like a proto-hippie. The novel derives its tension from the fact that there is a price to be paid for knowing Mary and one that Swithin rejects for the sake of his idealistic beliefs.

Mary's brother is a revolutionary leftist who proposes violence as a political tool and tries to co-opt Swithin into his group. Swithin refuses to renounce his belief in the artist being apolitical, loses Mary as a consequence and eventually dies in an accident.

The novel disappeared without a trace, the *Times Literary Supplement* alone giving it a formal notice. 'The story of Swithin Chance, who has a romantic and unreal air for all that, is related soberly and with quiet confidence. Swithin had high ideals, a sensitive soul and a great desire to be rich and therefore immune from the squalid struggle of life. Destiny, unkind at first, resolved his problem.'

Like most novels, Helen Ferguson's are the dated products of their time, of interest to the reader only as a development in the flowchart leading towards the work of Anna Kavan. They are small achievements, lacking the commercial hook necessary to bring them a substantial readership; they sparkle with imagination and compelling imagery, but ultimately they were lost among the skyscraper stacks of forgotten novels written in the twentieth century. Three of the six, *A Charmed Circle*, *Let Me Alone* and *A Stranger Still*, have been reprinted by Peter Owen under the name of Anna Kavan, while the other three have become scarcities commanding high prices among dealers and highly valued by Kavan enthusiasts. But ultimately the Helen Ferguson novels, unlike those of Anna Kavan, are no better or worse than those of her literary contemporaries, although submerged in their restraint there are signs of the extreme individuality she was to invent as an act of defiant liberation.

Money was not an issue for Helen Ferguson – the Edmonds were comfortable – so she was allowed to follow her own learning curve as a writer. Initially a painter, she had come over the years to prioritize writing as her primary expression; this shift seems to have stemmed from her experience of breakdown and the realization that literature was the mode of expression best suited to voicing her inner crises.

In 1938, when she emerged from her second period of hospitalization into a Europe under imminent threat of war, she did what she had been secretly contemplating for a long time: she became somebody else. The trio of Helen Woods, Helen Ferguson and Helen Edmonds were dead personae, never to be revisited. They were crash-test dummies left behind after impact. The new person who emerged carrying the name of the heroine of two of her novels was free to begin a new literary career and for the next few years to travel the world in the attempt to beat her addiction.

5

Blonde Ambition

*

HELEN FERGUSON'S ADOPTION of the alias Anna Kavan in 1938 brought a completion to the radical change of identity she had been contemplating ever since she toyed with the idea of becoming incognito and changing her name to Arlen, as early as 1926.

It is possible that she took the name Anna from the heroine of Tolstoy's *Anna Karenina* – one of the books she had been reading at The Elms shortly before her breakdown – and that Kavan, a Czech name, was a variant on the more common spelling Cavan, the K linking her pseudonymously to the writer she most admired, Franz Kafka, whose novel *The Castle*, translated by Edwin and Willa Muir, had been published in the same year.

She drew on her experiences during her second period in a sanatorium in the summer of 1938 for the book she was writing, called appropriately *Asylum Piece*. This work radically separated her from Helen Ferguson's fiction just as her new identity removed her from her past as the Helen Edmonds who loved bulldogs and the serenity of life in the Chilterns.

On her release from the clinic Anna moved into a friend's flat in Battersea. Remembering how well they had hit it off right from their first meeting in Bledlow Cross, she contacted her old friend Rhys Davies, who was then living in Maida Vale. When they met for tea Davies was at first completely thrown by the changes in Anna's physical appearance.

> One day a letter arrived from her. We were both living in London, and when I kept the arranged meeting I failed to recognise the woman running to me from under the trees of one of those suburban estates of dwellings. Helen Ferguson had vanished. This spectral woman, attenuated of body and face, a former abundance of auburn hair shorn and changed to metallic gold, thinned hands,

restless, was so different that my own need to readjust to her was a strain. She had not long been discharged from her second period in a hospital, and later I came to understand why she called one of her Anna Kavan books *I Am Lazarus*. She herself had returned from an abeyance of personality in the shades. The Lazarus myth always attracted her.

Rhys Davies was a confirmed homosexual writer, the son of a small village grocer in Clydach Vale, a tributary valley of the Rhondda. He shared in common with Anna that they were both born in 1901, but more importantly he found an additional affinity in that as writers they were both predominantly concerned with employing poetic imagery to describe their characters' inner states. In Rhys Davies, who lived precariously from writing but dressed as a dandified habitué of the Café Royal, Anna found a lifelong friend whose support was to prove invaluable to her survival on every level. Initially there was competition between the two, as is evident in 'The Summons' from *Asylum Piece*, in which Anna writing in the first person expresses jealousy at the ascendant reputation of 'R' while at the same time confirming the solid basis of their friendship. 'I still felt that a close and indestructible understanding existed between R and myself: an understanding which had its roots in some fundamental character similarity and was therefore exempt from the accidents of change.'

In 1939 Anna met Ian Hamilton, with whom she was to travel extensively in the early war years, when Hamilton's sister Margery began an affair with Stuart Edmonds. The conscientious objector Hamilton was an English expatriate who had returned to his birthplace from New Zealand hoping to score a hit with his anti-war three-act play *Falls the Shadow*, a work he had written in 1936, correctly assessing the escalating momentum of the Nazi war effort. A socialist who was in effect a remittance man, Hamilton was well educated and from a wealthy British family. The two travelled widely in countries that were still at peace, united in their attempt to outdistance the war, taking in Norway, New York and Mexico before living for a time in La Jolla, California. The story of their sojourn there in a beach house found its way into Kavan's novella *My Soul in China*.

In 1940 Rhys Davies introduced Anna to the theatre critic Raymond Marriott, who was also gay and who, despite a brief lapse in their friendship in the early 1950s, when Kavan broke with both George Bullock and Marriott, was to remain like Rhys Davies a totally dependable friend for life. Eventually he became her lodger, confidant and support, occupying the lower floor at Hillsleigh Road in the 1960s.

Anna's re-created identity coincided with a shift in her sexual orientation. She showed little interest in forming relationships after 1940, preferring instead to cultivate the friendship of homosexuals or to bond platonically in her relations with the likes of Ian Hamilton and Dr Bluth. Two failed marriages had left her sceptical of the need for relationships, and as an attractive woman who needed to be admired for her intelligence, studied appearance and gesturally camp aesthetic she gathered around her a small group of gay men connected to the arts who not only competed for her attention but brought her the rewards of colourful friendship without the onerous necessity for sex.

What Anna's serious breakdown had not done was to wipe out her creativity, and shortly after taking off on her globe-hopping wartime travels she published the brilliantly original *Asylum Piece* (1940), the first of her books to be published under the alias Anna Kavan. This was a collection of short pieces that shared in common the themes of breakdown, rehabilitation and the attendant paranoia that comes with being locked up and then ejected into a world where most people appear minatory. In an echo of Kafka, her characters are designated by initials rather than names, so giving them a greater degree of anonymity.

Nothing in Helen Ferguson's work had suggested the stripped-down method and the naked poetic eye with which she captures detail in *Asylum Piece*. All the unnecessary assemblage and character referents of the conventional novel are discarded in the interest of a new minimalism. All the stories apart from the title piece are told directly in the first person. For the first time she risked making the subjective, autobiographical element of her life the focal point, and the fictionalized reportage of her confinement is also her way of owning up to madness in both herself and others. Helen Edmonds was implicated by marriage and social conditioning in the domesticity of an uneventful Home Counties life, but Anna Kavan was reborn European, and much of *Asylum Piece*, which is set in Switzerland, gives its author a peculiarly anational feel, as though in reinventing herself she no longer owned to a specific nationality.

Having been locked away, no matter how comfortably, at the instigation of her husband, Anna turned her life round by converting institutionalization with its implied social stigma and clinical regime into a writing in which small gestures of compassion and defiance compensate for the neglect or indifference the patients experience on the part of the staff and those who have had them confined. In

'Asylum Piece VI' Anna provides us with a description of the room she occupied during her stay at the sanatorium.

> The room is quite large and has a parquet floor and well-proportioned furniture of pale wood; although one would not call it luxurious, it is certainly comfortable and pleasant. All the same, there is something a little odd, a little disquieting, about it. It would be difficult to locate the source of this impression; perhaps the circumstance that there is not a single hook anywhere, that all planes are bare and smooth, and that the electric light is protected by a wire screen, has something to do with it. The big window, too, is covered by a grille of wrought iron work which, though it is ornamental, suggests a utilitarian purpose.

Asylum Piece was brought out by Helen Ferguson's old publisher Jonathan Cape in 1940, at an infelicitous time for books, and was largely lost on account of the war. In the book's hallucinated scenarios Anna had picked up unconsciously on the influence of surrealism prevalent in European art and literature at the time, although with a few exceptions such as David Gascoyne, Roland Penrose and to a lesser extent Graham Sutherland the movement had largely been resisted in Britain. In fact, on the strength of her use of symbolic expression in *Asylum Piece*, and even more clearly her later book from the 1940s *Sleep Has His House*, Anna was more than any of her British contemporaries becoming directly linked to the European avant-garde, with its confessional mode of expression that sanctified madness as legitimate subject matter for art.

Asylum Piece was a critical success. Kafka's translator, Edwin Muir, called its author a writer of 'unusual imaginative power'. Writing in the *Sunday Times*, Sir Desmond MacCarthy noted:

> If *Asylum Piece* is not based on actual experience it is certainly an astonishing achievement . . . What is remarkable is that the subject matter of these stories not only kept the lamp alight in the fog of, at any rate, impending insanity, but was able to project dramatically the experience of fellow sufferers. That is just what the really insane can never do . . . there is a beauty about these stories which has nothing to do with their pathological interest, and is the result of art. Two or three, if signed by a famous name, might rank among the story-teller's memorable achievements. There is beauty in the stillness of the author's ultimate despair.

Alongside Virginia Woolf, Djuna Barnes, Anaïs Nin and Jean Rhys, Anna Kavan was beginning to earn recognition as a female artist whose work was centred not only on resistance to male oppression, but on the altogether bigger issue taken up similarly by George Orwell of defending the individual from all forms of totalitarianism.

By the time *Asylum Piece* was published Anna had already left wartime Britain behind. For the next three years she carried her art of self-redefinition to extremes as she trafficked across altered shipping lanes in the attempt to burn out her past, kick her habit and turn her back on the war.

6
On the Road

*

HAT WE KNOW of Anna Kavan's peripatetic life during the war years 1939–42, when she travelled extensively and became involved alternately with a young New Zealander called Ian Hamilton and an affluent American called Charles Fuller, is to be found in 'The Cactus Sign', an unpublished and strictly autobiographical account, running to five hundred pages, of rootless years of attempted heroin withdrawal and restlessly moving across the face of the globe. She left this manuscript in the possession of Charles Fuller, who was resident at the time at 40 East 52nd Street, New York City.

In these pages she expressed her final, heartfelt reproach directed at Stuart Edmonds:

> The man I was married to at the time did not come with me to the clinic. He was playing in a cricket match that day, so he sent me to the clinic with his brother's secretary in a hired car, a very old Daimler. I had given everything I had to that man for a long time. He, however, did not telephone to find out how I was. He never once enquired about me and quite soon abandoned me altogether.

In a revealing paragraph, subsequently erased, she comments on the ill-timed publication of *Asylum Piece*.

> Poor Jonathan Cape. Over a period of years he published my unsuccessful work. He did it because he believed in me as a writer. At last I did produce something really good, something quite out of the ordinary, if I say it myself. The preliminary reviews were first rate and everything seemed set for success. You've really brought it off this time, Jonathan said. Then the war started. That was the end of that.

Just how much Anna Kavan wrote, usually without attempting to publish the finished work, is clear from the fact that she completed the 90,000-word novella *My Soul in China*, mapping the catastrophic break-up of her second marriage, shortly after *Asylum Piece* and probably contemporaneously with the unpublished account of her wartime travels. Writing was the only occupation that gave her an identity, and she pursued it compulsively, as though her art was her only link to sanity. In a profoundly revealing commentary in 'We Know All the Answers' from 'The Cactus Sign', she points not only to her beginnings as a writer but provides rare autobiographical insight into her method of writing as a means of asserting some sort of control over reality.

> I was writing about what was happening to me. I've always been like that, having to tell people everything, about external events, but mostly about the things that go on inside myself. Until I was grown up I used to do it by talking. I used to relate long stories dramatizing the situation, and of course I was always in trouble for telling lies. When I was twenty-two I started writing it all down in a book which was more satisfactory. I've been doing that ever since.
>
> Lots of the things that happen to me I really can't bear at all. Then I write about them. Only just, mind you. But it makes that little difference. I suppose it gives one the illusion of having some control over things, of being somebody, instead of merely an anonymous grain of sand in the desert called chance.

Most people in a relationship with a writer complain of feeling to some degree excluded, left out while their partner lives out an antisocial pattern of being somewhere else – probably off limits – most of the time. Anna is quick to defend herself against similar criticism. She probably has Ferguson, Edmonds, Hamilton, Fuller and maybe others in mind when, writing from Bali, she writes of her self-doubt and of the sometimes negative reaction her writing engendered.

> I've had a lot of adverse criticism about the habit of writing everything down. There are the people who criticize me as if they were speaking purely for my own good. What they say is, how can you give yourself away like that in front of us all? So unrestrained and undignified. Then there are the people who accuse me of betraying confidences and of being disloyal towards friends. And then there are the ones who get personal and who want to know who the hell I think I am, anyway, that people should be interested in my reactions to the extent of

60,000 words or whatever it happens to be. I must admit that I'm inclined to sympathize with the last group.

H used to tell me that I'd never write a really first-class book until I stopped writing subjectively and began to write about subjects of general interest. No single individual, he kept saying, however complex could be sufficiently absorbing in themselves to hold the reader's attention. Perhaps he was right. I don't know. All I know is that I have to write in the way I feel, and that it is perfectly OK for anyone not to read my books if he or she doesn't want to.

In part she seems to be vindicating her habit of writing for long periods each day, a practice that deeply irritated Charles Fuller, making him fearful that she was using him as her subject. Like Anna's two husbands, Fuller was an alcoholic; he drank copious amounts of Old Highland whisky, vermouth and Gilbey's dry gin and chain-smoked Chesterfields bought in square tins. Anna, too, was drinking heavily at the time to support her attempted withdrawal from heroin; she seems to have had a preference for large pink gins. Her work on the extensive manuscript that evolved from her travels suggests that owing to the enervating strain of getting clean she was avoiding imaginative fiction of the nature of *Asylum Piece* and engaging with a writing that is stripped down, factual and strictly realistic. 'The Cactus Sign' resembles a series of opportunistic snapshots, part travelogue, part therapy, in that the intention is to record events almost as though in a diary and only in rare instances to colour them lightly with fiction. A combination of withdrawal, acute insecurity over the future and the probable danger of the ships she travelled on being the target of submarine activity brought about a crisis in Anna's creativity that caused her, in effect, to go naked.

She began her travels, wearing her Loden coat with a hood and quilted lining, by accompanying Ian Hamilton to Norway. She had a burning desire to reach China ultimately, a metaphor of the elusive country she would never in fact visit. Hamilton also accompanied her to California, where they occupied a beach cottage, an interlude in her life described in *My Soul in China*. Together they visited Carmel, but the lack of commitment on Hamilton's part did little to correct Anna's black moods and terrifying sense of insecurity. Staying at the Sir Francis Drake Hotel in San Francisco, and faced with Hamilton's decision to return to New Zealand, Anna found herself up on the fourteenth floor 'trying to decide whether to walk out of the window or to swallow a large number of sleeping pills which I kept by me for this sort of emergency'.

It was there in the bar of the Sir Francis Drake Hotel, in a state of disintegration, that she fortuitously met Charles Fuller, the American who was to companion her on her journey across the Pacific – the Atlantic sea-routes were closed to passenger ships on account of the war – with the express intention of visiting her family in South Africa. According to Anna she fell in love with Charles Fuller from the moment she saw him across the bar, not realizing that he was already otherwise committed. Their relationship was far from stable. Anna soon discovered that the gold fish he wore on a chain around his neck, to which he was greatly attached, was a talisman that had been given him by his girlfriend. When the ship stopped at Cebu in the tropics Anna waded out into the sea wearing a blue silk dress and later that night took a large dose of Luminal and four sodium amytal tablets and passed out for twenty-four hours. The ship's doctor was called, and after being violently sick she recovered consciousness.

After visa problems at Macassar Anna travelled on in the company of Fuller to Batavia – a place she found just another species of boredom. Fired up with whisky, Fuller found the courage to tell her that although he was in love with somebody else he would take care of her practically and financially for the next six months. Anna was now forty, and Fuller's limited offer was an intolerable reminder of the loneliness of her condition as a woman alone in a world eclipsed by war.

They played deck tennis between bouts of heavy drinking. They stopped off at Singapore, the nearest Anna got to China, but she found that the brutally hyperactive pace of the city only exacerbated her shot nerves. They boarded the SS *Plancius*, its portholes blacked out, for Surabaya. They had an altercation there, and Anna threatened to board the *New Holland* alone for Australia, but they patched things up sufficiently to take the SS *Merak* together to Bali. Anna recorded that she had crossed the equator for the third time in two weeks without ever once feeling 'any bump when we went over that line which is marked 0 on the maps'.

In Bali they stayed in a hotel that resembled a string of bamboo cabins. Anna found this environment more conducive to enduring her withdrawal symptoms than the frenetic speed of Singapore. Sitting on her veranda overlooking the dark-blue Indian Ocean, dressed in shorts on account of the heat or sunbathing nude on a deserted beach, she wrote her way through the days, leaving Fuller paranoid that he was the subject of the words she committed to a liver-coloured notebook.

Anna's inveterate insomnia seems to have troubled her deeply on her travels, and her intake of alcohol only intensified the problem. Lying awake night after night in the tropical heat, and unable to disengage from the continuous brain-noise generated by her inner dialogue, she longed to find refuge in the normal quotient of sleep. 'When I think of the way other people can sleep the only suit-able retort seems to be death; I feel then that I want to die, just as you might feel you want a cup of coffee.' The problem remained with her for the rest of her life, another symptom of her inexhaustible anxiety. She used sleeping pills like Luminal and Nembutal intermittently, but she disliked the side-effects and the way they furred her creative energies.

They remained in Bali throughout the dry season and at night listened anx-iously to broadcasts from San Francisco giving accounts of the persistent air raids devastating London. Anna was particularly concerned about her London flat and presumably her son Bryan's welfare, but at the same time she refused to make war and its propagandist spin the subject of her writing. Instead she con-cerned herself with noting curiosities of Balinese cuisine, such as the local habit of eating fried dragonflies, or musing on her peculiar fixation with mirrors. Given the importance of mirrors as metaphors for seeing and being seen, her comments on their place in her life are particularly significant.

> The consequence of it all was that life became impossible for me without at least two long mirrors in every room. Believe it or not, those mirrors were absolutely essential to me. I had one fixed up where the light was strongest and another so that I could view myself somewhat more leniently. I ask you, was that any way in which to live? Can you require so many long mirrors in your life and remain a reasonable being?

Living out of suitcases was hard; so, too, was the fractiousness of a relation-ship sustained by alcohol as a mood regulator, shot through with resentment on Anna's part and desperation on Fuller's. She was doing her best to cultivate the art of what she called 'non-attachment', an expedient brought about by rejection-sensitivity and the need not to feel dependent in relationships. Things reached a crisis in September and the two resolved to separate, intending to travel together on an inter-island steamer to Surabaya and from there to Batavia, where Anna would book a passage on the *Straat Sunda* bound for Africa and Fuller would go the opposite way back to New York.

Secretly Anna noted that she missed the little luxuries that were part of her existence back home and wrote of her longing to go out and buy Stravinsky records, a bottle of Bois des Iles, expensive bath salts, new dresses, white flowers and smoked salmon.

They took a cattle boat to Surabaya, the cows standing in rows on the deck. Anna was growing increasingly despondent at the signs of Fuller's elation that he had started his journey home. At Surabaya they switched ships and headed for Semarang in Java. At this time Anna returned to fiction to write the story 'One of the Hot Spots', about a man who jumps overboard fully dressed with his leather shoes on but thinks better of drowning himself and clambers back up the ship's rail and returns to his cabin. The story, written at a time when she felt betrayed and totally alone in the world, when she was using her writing as a sanity-preserving survival tactic, could arguably be read as a metaphor for her father's suicide.

The *Plancius* stopped off for a day in Batavia, and Anna and Fuller ended up doing some serious drinking on the terrace of the Hotel des Indes, where they were joined by a group of European men equally intent on getting wasted. A drunken party ensued at the hotel, from which Anna escaped to a night club with a man called Joe after glasses had been smashed and the atmosphere turned nasty. It was one of many scenes of drunken chaos that marked the emotional friction of an ultimately barren relationship. In a scratched-out note written at the time, Anna stated that she wished she had the facility to describe turbulent bar room scenes in the manner of Hemingway, so as to give them more authenticity.

Fuller clearly felt guilty about his double life. He attempted to make a compromise in the interest of peace by offering to take Anna with him to the USA providing she made no demands on him emotionally.

> To begin with, he said, you've got to accept the fact that I'm in love with someone else, and that I'm not going to let anything interfere with that, so that I can't possibly be emotionally responsible for you. I'll be practically responsible for you as far as I can. I'll see that you have enough money. And somewhere to live. And a chance to make good. And of course I'll be with you as much as possible. But essentially you'll be alone.

This offer promised Anna some temporary security, as well as asylum from a war-ravaged Europe, but it did little to reprieve her sense of abandonment. With two failed marriages behind her, and facing the prospect of visiting her recently remarried mother, the woman she saw as the source of her psychological damage, Anna had every reason to feel dispossessed. Her only small income at the time came from books, leaving her dependent on Fuller to pay her way, an unenviable situation for a woman resolved to cultivate detachment. She was acutely aware that her quest for unconditional freedom was a defence mechanism on her part, rather than a natural instinct growing out of the need to be indifferent and alone.

Non-attachment is admirable, it never lets you down; it's the one thing worth aiming at, but it's impracticable. It's too good for people like me. It's too exalted for any human being who's messed up with all the crazy emotions I get messed up with from time to time. It's too cold for persons who like sitting in bars, who must have sunshine, who must have contact, who cannot live indefinitely without touching other human beings and loving them, their old clothes and the way their hair blows up in the wind.

But detachment and a coolness bordering on anhedonia were Anna's only way of continuing to be with a man who made it very clear that he was unwilling to commit.

A visit to the American consulate in Batavia resulted in Anna being refused a visa to enter the USA for six months or a year, owing to discrepancies with her passport arising from the fact that she was born not in Britain but in Cannes. She was advised by the consulate not to return to America but to continue with her plan of travelling to Africa. After persistence on her part she was granted the concession of a six-day transit visa, which she accepted in the hope that it would be extended on her arrival in the USA.

Fuller was waiting for money to be transferred from his bank so that he could give Anna $500 with which to enter the USA, so they made an excursion to Singapore, sailing there on a cargo boat called the *Odense* across the Java Sea. For the second time the city frayed her nerves with its congested streets and crazy upbeat night life. At night, Anna noted, 'the air was a narcotic, full of stupefaction and neutral dreams'.

When Fuller's money arrived they left the urban recklessness of Singapore and sailed for Belawan, where the translucent yellow water swarmed with jellyfish. They took a train through solid jungle heat from there to Medan and Brastagi, a hill station 1,800 metres above the sea, where they slept outside under the stars, grateful for the cool high air.

From Brastagi they journeyed on to Balik Papan in Borneo, the last port of call before the ship began its 12,000-mile trek across the Pacific. To Anna the whole journey was starting to take on the unreal qualities of film. Her constant state of nervous anxiety and dissociation from events, not to mention her cellular craving for heroin, left her panicky and feeling disconnected. At Balik Papan she made an attempt to reconnect with the life going on around her, reminding herself of the need to enter more fully into experience. 'It was then that I realised how the lifestream writes everything in the world. How the splendour of the whole world is one. The only thing you must do to take part in the splendour is to live, and not die. Looking at Balik Papan, tasting again the bad taste in my mouth like blood, I was glad I was there as a part of the living stream.'

Despite the possibility that the *Odense*, which was transporting a valuable cargo of oil and rubber, might be sunk by a submarine, Anna felt surprisingly safe at sea, temporarily relieved from having to make practical decisions about her future. Being at sea was her way of taking time out. Sitting alone in a cane chair on the deck, eating oranges and watching the endlessly changing cloud formations arrange and rearrange themselves in sculptural patterns overhead, she felt insulated from the material reality that she so feared. She and Fuller were the only passengers on the 10,000-ton *Odense*, surrounded by the vastness of the blue Pacific, and the war and its catastrophes, leaking through the ship's radio, dissolved into unreality in Anna's mind. She noted the impossibility of making real the idea of the civilian casualties in the nightly air raids on London and how inconceivable it was that friends were numbered among the dead.

This sense of security evaporated when they arrived at Panama City, where the ship was delayed for two days. Impatient to get home, Fuller decided to fly to New York, leaving Anna on board the *Odense* to complete the journey by sea. With only $100 and a transit visa in her possession, Anna spent the remaining week of the voyage consumed by the fear that Fuller would renege on his promise to meet her and stand security for her in the USA.

On her arrival in New York on 26 October 1940 Anna managed to get her visa extended to sixty days. She was introduced into Charles Fuller's bohemian circle, with whom she smoked liberal quantities of marijuana. Among others she met the photographer Walker Evans, whose uncredited photograph of her as a blonde, highly stylized, perfectly made-up woman with thin pencilled eyebrows and a smile manufactured for the lens was, much to her dismay, to be displayed on the dust jacket of nearly all her books published in the UK.

Under huge strain owing to the inevitability of Charles Fuller's imminent marriage, Anna none the less made her new book *Asylum Piece* known to George Davis, the fiction editor of *Harper's Bazaar*, who published three chapters from it in the magazine; this ensured her a small reputation in America throughout the 1940s. The Editor's Guest Book recorded her visit to the magazine's offices:

> Anna Kavan came to see us straight off the boat from Bali. She had started for South Africa to join her mother then unpredictably turned about mid trip – drifted vaguely back to New York and appeared in our office, a blonde blue-eyed young English woman, book in hand. *Asylum Piece*, from which we have picked three chapters, was published in England in 1940 by Jonathan Cape. She wrote her first book in Burma at the age of twenty and has had six published since. We were not surprised to find that Miss Kavan had sailed for New Zealand before this issue went to press.

She remained in a snowbound New York, in which the diamond-pointed air was almost too cold to breathe, until January 1941, when she left on a steamer bound via the Panama Canal for New Zealand and a rendezvous with the other equally enigmatic man in her life, Ian Hamilton.

7

Falling Off the Edge of the World

*

In late January 1941 Anna Kavan sailed via the Panama Canal to Fiji, where she was granted a transit visa before taking passage to Auckland in New Zealand. The reasons for her going there are obscure. On the rebound from Charles Fuller, she ostensibly made the journey to join Ian Hamilton in Auckland, knowing in advance that Hamilton would offer her no more commitment than Fuller. Something of Anna's untouchable allure – she was after all seeking a platonic relationship – is illustrated by the fact that both Fuller and Hamilton became deeply involved with her on an emotional level, while accepting the non-physical parameters she imposed on their relations.

A secondary reason for the decision to visit New Zealand may well have been, as David Callard suggests, an attempt to distance herself from supplies of heroin. She was on the run from the tyranny of white powders that trafficked her veins, and the absence of all mention of drugs in 'The Cactus Sign' suggests that she was making serious attempts to conquer her habit. 'The Cactus Sign' is in some ways Kavan's alcoholic book, its pages registering her heavy intake of pink gin, whisky and vermouth during the days spent in stifling ship's cabins and nights in jazzy night clubs in foreign ports. The undercurrent of reckless hysteria in her relationships with both Fuller and Hamilton was mediated by the volatility of liquor and not the chilled-out cool of heroin.

Before setting sail for New Zealand Anna had forwarded her new novel, *Change the Name*, to Jonathan Cape for publication in 1941. This was the second book to be published under the alias Anna Kavan. It incorporated experience drawn from her travels in the Far East, as well as remixing the constituents of her failed marriage to Stuart Edmonds with fine descriptive writing evoking the rural setting at Bledlow Cross.

At her most vulnerable, Anna wrote without embellishment of the process of simply staying alive by remaining outside the official war zone. She was effectively redundant to the war effort, a supernumerary faced with the degrading prospect of being valueless to the military. Frustrated by the inevitable confusion created by her French birth, she retaliated by rounding on the authorities. With her customary paranoia, she wrote *en route* to New Zealand, 'In wartime a civilian, unless he happens to be in with the big shots, is just a kind of low organism only permitted to exist for the purpose of filling up forms and being taxed and bullied and pushed around generally.' This had been her experience during her extensive wartime travels, and perhaps by going to somewhere as remote as New Zealand she felt she was removing herself totally from a civilization in which she no longer believed. Her ambivalent feelings about New Zealand and its inhabitants are expressed in a 1943 *Horizon* article, 'New Zealand: Answer to an Inquiry', and in the account she kept of her time there in 'The Cactus Sign'.

Most of Anna's time in New Zealand was spent living with Ian Hamilton at Waitahanui, a small village in Torbay, then the quasi-bohemian and least inhabited of Auckland's east coast bays. According to Hamilton she wrote every day in her new environment, screening herself from the world with an intense absorption in her work. Hamilton's social group in Auckland included the leftist lawyer Frank Haigh and his wife Honey, the architect Vernon Brown, the photographer Clifton Firth and the exiled poet Karl Wolfskehl, all of whom are drawn into Anna's reconstruction of her time spent at Torbay. It is possible, too, that Anna met the egotistical New Zealand writer Frank Sargeson, a man who shared literary and political affinities with Hamilton and who in later life recalled how Hamilton and Kavan cruised about the North Shore in a black sedan, reminding him of 'a Chicago mobster and his moll'. Anna recorded realistic impressions of the place in 'The Cactus Sign', seeing it with journalistic precision.

> There are wooden shacks, called baches, with tin roofs most of them, some unpainted, some half-painted, having names like Itledo and Havarest and Dewdropin. Most of them look like as if they had been knocked together by amateur builders at weekends, and every weekend there is hammering in Waitahanui, some new enthusiast in the building line starting up. Nowhere in Waitahanui is there any place where alcohol can be bought, but as against this it must be recorded that the post office store provides soft drinks in a wondrous range of colours, as well as choc-bons, and ice creams in cartons and cones . . .

Her stripped-down reportage of her time in New Zealand is as basic as the country she was exploring. Her descriptions are less cohesive than the detailed record of her travels with Charles Fuller and perceived without the imaginative colouring textured into *My Soul in China*, but Anna none the less brings her novelist's eye to bear on indigenous customs and the eccentricities of the locals.

She was denied a permit to travel by rail and hampered by the wartime petrol shortage, but she made a car journey with Hamilton, sharing the driving, in an old black Chevrolet from Auckland to Napier – a distance of about three hundred miles over a network of badly pot-holed pumice roads. The purpose of the journey was to visit Hamilton's mother who was ill in hospital. They drove in blinding tropical rainstorms at night through the high bush covering the hills. The dark outside was solid, and Anna felt threatened by an isolation that was almost palpable. 'I turned round once and looked out of the back window and the darkness was like a hole in the universe.' Having set out at four in the afternoon they arrived at half past eight in Rotorua, a town full of geysers and hot springs, and managed to get a room at the hotel and, better still for Anna, Martini cocktails at the bar. They resumed their journey in the morning through subsided earthquake country with cold rain studding the Chevy's windshield. It was still raining when they arrived at the hill town of Napier; Anna had neglected to bring her fur coat and was almost immobilized by the brutally debilitating cold. They took rooms in a hotel looking out at the adjacent snow-peaked hills, the days alternating between rain and a cold brilliant as a blue diamond. Anna noted with her unfailing facility for natural description that she would remember 'the hills, not very far off, and exceedingly crumpled like a piece of very old tissue paper, with the snow on them; and in front of them the flat plain that was once the sea bottom, the sea floor unceremoniously shoved up by an earthquake into the light of day'.

When Hamilton's mother seemed certain of recovery, the two managed to persuade a sympathetic fuel controller in Napier to give them twenty gallons of petrol to make the return journey to Auckland. They drove back through hills littered with truncated forests and in parts matted with rata, totara, rimu, lancewood, punga, fivefinger and other varieties of bush vegetation. They stopped in transit at Huntly, where the local coal miners were on strike, a place Anna was glad to leave behind on account of its ugliness, before hauling the petrol-guzzling Chevy back to Auckland. In Auckland Anna again encountered passport problems. Her dilemma was that in order to get to South Africa as her final destination, it was necessary to travel via the Panama Canal, and it was mandatory even on a

British ship to have an American visa, the very document that Anna was repeatedly denied.

Partly relieved by the temporary reprieve afforded her by the discrepancy in her papers, Anna and Hamilton stocked up on food and took the ferry back to Waitahanui, where the house had been left untouched and Anna to her relief discovered her fur coat still on its hanger, together with all her permanently unpacked travelling bags stashed like old friends around her room. The houses in Waitahanui merited Anna's attention: they were wooden, tin-roofed, one-storey shacks, with rainwater tanks and a more or less total absence of plumbing, although there was electricity for lighting and cooking. Writing about Waita-hanui in her *Horizon* piece, Anna disparaged the obsolete ferries, inconvenient, expensive, infrequent and dangerous in bad weather. Nor did the local cooking meet with her approval: 'There is no place where you can eat (except ice creams at the store), but this is not much loss as NZ cooking, except in the best hotels, is rather regrettable, having most of the characteristics of the worst sort of English cooking with the addition of strong cups of tea all through the day.'

Anna was acutely conscious of being an outsider and reacted badly to the initial hostility that the locals showed strangers. She resented their lack of culture and the stereotypical gender roles expected of both sexes, the men getting together in drinking parties and the women confined to domestic chores.

Waitahanui is situated on a rocky coast with access to a number of sandy beaches and bays and commands a view over a raft of inshore islands and reefs; the place impressed Anna with its natural beauty. Inland, hilly scrub country was intercut with pine plantations and farmland. The roads were poor and the village offered no other amenities than a store, a post office and a church that held fort-nightly services. She liked the antediluvian landscapes but disliked the people and found even Auckland provincial and without any cultural stimulus. She wrote in *Horizon*:

> What you may call the *leitmotif* of all this is a quiet parochial slowness. People wander up and down the main streets staring into the windows of shops that are full of agricultural implements and meat pies. Everything's shut, there's noth-ing to do except go to the pub or the cinema or, if it happens to be the right day, to the races. No music, no theatres, no pictures except an occasional exhibition of local talent, no magazines of what's termed cultural interest.

As she had done with Charles Fuller, she and Ian Hamilton drank to alleviate the boredom. That the relationship had made disturbing inroads into Hamilton's emotional resources is apparent from Anna's attempt to re-vision it in *My Soul in China*. Hamilton's belief that he had been used by Anna, and twisted in the process, is given powerful expression.

'You've turned me into a criminal by depending on me all the time. I reckon it's the worst crime you can commit to put your personality over somebody else. Even if you stop them boozing or taking dope, you're only putting a worse dope in front of them. A person's got to be independent – a conscious, self-contained human being . . . I'm not the same as when I met you; I don't practise what I preach any longer. I tell you not to do things, and then I go and do them myself. You've turned me into a hypocrite. I know that's not a fair accusation, and the fact I can make it proves what you've done to me in the way of damage. But what the hell does it matter? I'm just a bloody mess – I've ballsed up several people's lives, my own included, to no purpose whatever.'

Even in a place as remote as Waitahanui they were not altogether free of the threat of war. Anna recounts how the Home Guard drove up in a small military truck one afternoon and began putting up barbed wire defences on the beach to prevent a Japanese landing. Looking out to sea and across at the Coromandel, with the islands of Rangitoto, Tiri-Tiri and The Noises dissolving in and out of view, Anna could not take the threat of a Japanese invasion seriously. She preferred to sunbathe naked on the white beaches fronting the translucently aquamarine Hauraki Gulf. In October Hamilton learnt that the appeals of men of his age group against military service were starting to be heard, and Anna received her passport with amended wording that would permit the American consul to issue her with a visa allowing her to travel to England via the Panama Canal within a month. A visit to the American consul involved a trip to Auckland. Their brief interlude away from the world threatened to come to an abrupt end. To Anna it was as though a glass screen protecting her from reality had shattered. In 'The Cactus Sign' she wrote, 'Our time at Waitahanui was coming close to its end, and we both wished this was not so. I've said nothing about it; but contemplating the end as we drove over the hills, I saw a queer shape slip through the manouka behind the sign called Lonely Track.' She was always on the look-out for signs that would create an interface between inner and outer worlds, and she interpreted the words Lonely Track as an indication of her future – a resumption of her solitary travels, the needle, alienation and the whole isolationist world she so feared.

It was a clear sunlit October day when they visited Auckland. Anna documents how she arrived at the American consulate and took the lift to the sixth floor, which gave her a panoramic view of the harbour complex outside the windows. The consul informed her with minimal protocol that a visa would be issued to her within twenty-four hours of the date on which she proposed to travel.

Warned of the dangers implicit in the journey, she returned by car with Hamilton to Waitahanui. The village had offered the offbeat, slightly zany social company of Honey and Frank as a relief from boredom, and Anna and Ian Hamilton had been regulars at their weekend drinking parties, but they, too, had now returned to Auckland. However, there were still other local eccentrics whom Anna had got to know, such as Lord Clarke, who lived in a derelict shack with a boarded-up shop front, the fascia containing a faded advertisement for Orange Crush, and who drove an original Model T Ford wearing a cape and crumpled grey Homburg. There was also the alcoholic Mr Porown, who had lost an arm in a sawmill accident and who in a drunken state had set fire to a letter from a London solicitor informing him of a substantial inheritance.

As October lengthened, the days grew hotter, and to Anna time seemed momentarily to stand still. 'Stalingrad was still holding out,' she wrote; 'nothing much seemed to be going on in the Middle East, hardly any news came through from the Americans fighting in the Solomons.' There were distractions, too, such as the local celebrations for Labour Day and the rumble of an army reconnaissance biplane rattling over at cliff level; but outwardly nothing intruded on their insular world, framed by the empty window of blue sea and blue sky.

On Friday 23 October Hamilton was summoned by post to attend an interview for enrolment in the Home Guard at No. 2 Armed Forces Appeal Board, 2nd Floor, Civic House, Queen Street, Auckland. It was Anna who collected the card from the post office. Hamilton had no chance of getting to Auckland for the appointment, which was that day, and in any case as a pacifist he felt tense and agitated at the prospect of his impending interview.

Anna records that she was at Waitahanui for the celebration of Labour Day on 26 October. Hamilton had got permission from a land agent to plant tomatoes in a gully on the outskirts of the village, and they spent the day cutting manouka stakes to support the plants. Hamilton did the cutting with a saw and chopper,

while Anna explored the adjoining countryside, which offered views of the coastline and the suburbs of Auckland in the distance. She walked in the direction of
Long Bay – 'the saddest beach I've ever walked upon' – bordered by tussocky sand
dunes and Vaughan's farm. The flat beach stretching under a thin white sky was an
appropriate place to walk, given her mood, the desolation of the landscape reinforcing her sense of loneliness and blues and of falling off the edge of the world.

Anna stayed on at Waitahanui throughout November, awaiting news of a
ship that would take her to Africa via England and understandably, given her
unmanageable anxiety, reluctant to leave Ian Hamilton. Knowing that her time
there was drawing to a close, she attached deeper significance to everything she
did, attempting to live directly in the moment as a means of consciously expanding time. The days appeared discontinuous, each one separated from the last and
made special by her investing it with an inventory of personal associations. But
the anxiety she felt over her imminent departure surfaced unconsciously in the
form of chronic insomnia. Her pattern, common to a lot of depressives, was to fall
asleep tired and wake up at two in the morning, unable to get back to sleep. She
was adamant, however, that she would rather suffer sleep deprivation than resort
to prescribed heavy-duty barbiturates. She neither read nor otherwise attempted
to distract herself in the long reaches of the night, but lay there quietly preoccupied with the endless brain-noise and inner stream of her thoughts.

In November there was welcome news that Rommel was on the defensive in
Egypt, information that coincided with a message from the Southern Cross Line
of a ship sailing to England in two weeks. Anna both welcomed the news and tried
to shut it out of her mind. The names of the ships she had travelled on and the
places she had visited were fast becoming a list-mantra she invoked as a means of
lyricizing her travels. In 'The Cactus Sign' she reminded herself of her principal
ports of call: Oslo, Acapulco, La Jolla, San Francisco, Manila, Macassar,
Surabaya, Batavia, Singapore, Kuta, Brastagi, New York, Los Angeles, Hono-
lulu, Pago Pago, Takapuna and Waitahanui. Associating places with specific
images fixed in her memory, she recalled the immediate past with brilliant poetic
virtuosity.

The past is security and all that: the past is the wall in Oslo with the rearing
horse on it; and the smiling faces and flowery streets of La Jolla, the little negro
boy selling *Saturday Evening Post* under the eucalyptus trees outside the post
office; and the pelicans diving at Passe-a-Grille. The past is masked Rangda

dancing her terrible island witch dance. The past is a steamer crossing a tropical ocean, an American leaning over the rail, myself beside him, travelling towards the present which is Waitahanui; which is about to become the past.

There was news not only of a Southern Cross Line ship travelling to England but also the rumour of a boat sailing direct to South Africa from a port in the Bay of Islands. To clarify the facts, Anna duly visited the Southern Cross Line in their waterfront Maritime Building in Auckland, a complex largely taken over by the military and naval authorities. There she was informed that the ship in question was due to sail in a week's time, much sooner than she had anticipated. She was additionally told not only that the boat was a degraded sluggish vessel, unlike their usual A class cargo boats, but that she would be the only woman on board and that due to the dangers inherent in such a voyage she travelled at her own risk.

Next she had to visit the American consulate in Auckland to procure the visa that would permit her to travel through the Panama Canal. Fingerprinted for security reasons, and made to fill out another plethora of forms, Anna eventually received her visa and was informed by the consulate that the ship sailed on Friday 13 November.

Her last days at Waitahanui were quiet, immeasurably sad ones, in which she and Ian Hamilton tried desperately hard to avoid the subject of her departure. Anna sat outside the house for hours on an old bench watching the rise and fall of the tide, coloured by the marine sky arching over the gulf, knowing that she had to go but reluctant to acknowledge it.

Hamilton had been the principal reason for her visiting New Zealand. She remained ambivalent about her feelings for the country itself, making it very clear in her *Horizon* article that while she found the natural landscape uplifting she remained singularly uninspired by the people and culture – shocked by what she perceived as their lack of an aesthetic. But, being Anna Kavan, she assimilated all the experience available there for use in future books. Something of the wide tracts of open scrub and the desolation of a volcanic landscape that she encountered on her dusty high-speed forays into the hills with Hamilton eventually found its way into the post-apocalyptic landscape of her later fiction, including the novels *Eagles' Nest* and *Ice*.

In her *Horizon* article she noted:

It seems fundamentally to be a place of formidable alien power and of animal and human life-negation. In my picture I see the endless will of the land to

shake off the intruders sparsely settled upon it and to return to its original sombre and silent aloofness, no mammal stirring under the grave, enormous antique
trees, no sounds but the sound of water and wind and the outlandish chiming of
bell birds in the vast antipodean bush. That's what I see, in my picture, of the
country New Zealand. Always the desolation, always the splendour, always the
loneliness, always the opposition, always the ancient trees, the birds which
inhabit no other country, the volcanic mountains, the mud bubbling and chuck-
ling. And always, everywhere, strangeness.

She was leaving New Zealand without prospects for the future. England was
at war and was anyhow associated in her mind with her shattered marriage, while
her intended destination South Africa was now home to her obsessively jealous
mother who had married the much younger and homosexual Hugh Tevis,
arguably to accommodate a lifestyle mediated by unlimited wealth. To Anna,
who lacked any reliable source of income, the possibility of receiving financial
assistance from her stepfather may have been the motive for the journey. Ian
Hamilton had provided her with a secure place and an unconditional relationship at a time when she most needed refuge. As far as we know, she was still off
heroin and would anyhow have found the drug difficult to pick up illegally in
New Zealand. Panicky about travel, she packed her luggage well in advance of
leaving and stared fixedly at the outline of her cases while lying awake in the
night. The day before she left she took a last long walk out to Long Bay, with
Vaughan's sheep grazing on the hills and the susurration of surf in the air, and
sat under the pines staring out at the sea.

8

A Woman Left Lonely

*

I T WAS A NATURALLY apprehensive
Anna Kavan, assiduously occupied with writing her journal as a stabilizing occupation, who set sail from Auckland on a boat called *The Wanderer* that first travelled leisurely down the coast for two days to Napier. For Anna the journey was like entering a discontinuous space-time, and she stayed up on deck, glad of the invigorating sea air, watching porpoises intermittently jump out of the serene lime-green sea.

She records a profound sense of loss and grief at the things she was leaving behind, not least the quiet beaches at Waitahanui, where she had pursued her love of sunbathing and bronzed her naked body in the relentless heat. She was returning on a reverse voyage that confronted her uncomfortably with her immediate past, and in Napier, feeling particularly insecure, she recalled Hamilton's attentiveness to her needs. 'Wherever I happened to go in the town or in the hotel H went with me. He was part of the dream that now was without a dreamer.' In a highly dissociated state of anxiety she attended a garden party at Napier given by one of Hamilton's friends, and she wrote of how on the way back at night in an interminable bus ride she experienced an altered state in which a gateway to the psychic world seemed to open, giving her access to other-dimensional consciousness. This beam of intuitive awareness was both disquieting and reassuring, an eruption of visionary experience into her solitary life at the time; episodes of being visited in this way are numerous in the development of her later fiction and short stories.

From Napier, *The Wanderer* sailed to Wellington, where she berthed for eight hours, but security did not permit anybody to go ashore. The harbour was full of US invasion barges, and Anna, with her novelistic eye for detail, observed crates of gas masks and respirators with mouthpieces stashed on the quay.

The Wanderer was the latest of a line of ships on which Anna had sailed, with evocative names such as *Black Watch, Kungsholm, City of Los Angeles, Jagersfontein, Plancius, Merak, Odense* and *Mariposa*, during her four voyages across the Pacific and two across the Atlantic. As she had been warned, *The Wanderer* was a slow cargo boat, twenty-six years old, dilapidated, given a lick of impermanent grey paint and carrying twelve passengers. The food was bad and the accommodation basic – the cabins were inundated with a complex network of pipes that provided dysfunctional plumbing and equally inadequate heating. Despite sharing little affinity with them, Anna was glad of the company of ten New Zealand sergeant pilots and one pilot officer who comprised the only other passengers on board.

Feeling totally alone in the world, and unused to the practicalities of coping, Anna worked at cultivating the psychological facility of ' non-attachment', a self-devised programme aimed at keeping her habitually detached from emotions. It was also a means of defence aimed at shutting out so much of what she feared about reality. She was hiding deep hurt at the time and learning to live behind the inscrutable, perfectly made-up and impenetrable face she presented to the world.

> The early part of the time I was on board *The Wanderer* was the first time in my adult life that I'd been absolutely alone, and I don't mean alone in the sense that applies all the time to people not at home in the world. I mean actually, factually alone, without anyone to whom I could even speak the words that were natural to me to speak, without as far as I could see the faintest possibility of human contact or communication.

Like all obsessives who identify with a particular mental state, Anna could not imagine a time when she would ever be free of this almost cryogenic human isolation. Locked into her obsession and without heroin as a palliative, she felt she had hit rock bottom. Her distressing sense of alienation on board reminded her of her school days, when she had experienced similar feelings of painful isolation and of belonging to another species.

The routine on board never varied. They rang a bell for meals and the passengers and crew convened in the saloon at three long tables wedged tightly together, reminding Anna of school dinner times. Everyone had an appointed place and sat down to face a serviette in a numbered ring. Anna wrote of how she hated the unbending discipline of the ship's officers all sitting at one table, while the passengers and crew sat at the other two. Out of loneliness she got into the habit of staying on after the others had left the table to keep the captain company. It was a little ritual she repeated each day, although the captain was not in the habit of making stimulating conversation.

The evenings were the worst time for Anna, for as soon as it got dark the black-out screens were put up and no natural light entered the cabins. Walking on deck was a precarious occupation owing to the clutter of machinery and the overspill of cargo. To someone as claustrophobic as Anna, being sealed below deck without access to an open window immediately triggered panic. Rather than be alone, she would join the other passengers in a fan-churned, chokingly hot smoking-room and attempt, despite the bad light, to read a book in one of the nine dilapidated easy chairs positioned around a centre table. The pilots amused themselves playing crown and anchor or draughts, drank spirits and listened to distorted jazz and blues on the crackly radio. Although the company was far from sympathetic, the distraction provided Anna with a necessary respite from her tediously solitary hours.

If the raucous masculinity she encountered in the smoking-room was an ordeal, she dreaded returning to her cabin for the night. Sleep was hard to come by. The uneven distribution of cargo made the ship roll violently, and there was the noise of the night watch pacing up and down in heavy boots overhead. Rather than be shunted from side to side all night by the ship's predictably rhythmic lurches, Anna devised a method of putting her lifebelt under the mattress and making an angle for herself to lie in between the bulkhead and the skewed mattress. It was a little piece of improvisation that actually worked, and, even if she didn't sleep and stayed awake reading the in-cabin emergency instructions, she was at least able to escape the destabilizing prospect of being jolted from side to side all night.

She described how she struck up a friendship with the first officer. The high point of her day came at noon, when the two would meet in the bar and drink English gin with tonic that 'was the last of the Singapore stuff'. Her midday drink with the young, unexpectedly sensitive chief officer became one of those rituals that make difficult circumstances tolerable. The two sat drinking unmeasured pink gins in the cupboard-sized bar each day until the lunch bell called them to the saloon.

Immersed in it, Anna noted the insufferable sense of ennui that gradually overtook the entire ship as they travelled north in the warm weather. There was nothing for the passengers to do but sunbathe on deck, and the crew were similarly bored on the open sea, often without occupation for long stretches.

Two days south of the equator there was the diversion of gun practice, an exercise designed to shake the crew out of their tropical lassitude. Anna had little or no interest in the performance of six-inch guns, twelve-pounders, Brownings, Hotchkisses and Chicago pianos, and she looked on with disinterest as the gunners excitedly closed in on their targets.

The voyage rapidly devolved into a sense of extended *déjà vu* as Anna revisited a succession of ports for the second time, arriving in the pouring rain at Balboa, a place that scared up memories of her visit there with Charles Fuller and of the whole volatile dynamic of their mercurial, incandescent on–off relationship.

From Balboa *The Wanderer* sailed through the Panama Canal to Colon, where they arrived late in the evening. In the steamy hot rain Anna took one of the launches ashore and explored the brimming town and its hectic nightlife. The place throbbed with bars, brothels, drunks and crazy traffic. There were American soldiers everywhere packing the riotous bars and late-night bluesy nightclubs that were systematically patrolled by the military police. Accompanied by the ship's captain she drank Panamanian Scotch until 5 a.m. in the Tropico, the Atlantico, the Florida, the Congo and several other torrid basements in which music blared out of the jukebox.

The next night ashore, wearing a bright red nail-varnish called Chili Bean, Anna accompanied the chief officer to Bilgray's, one of the classier bars in town that boasted a dense tropical garden with flame trees. The pair recognized each other's inherent nervousness – Anna had a habit of constantly fidgeting with her hands – and an intimacy developed between them, allowing them both to open up with reserve about their private lives. Anna appreciated the chief officer's cool as the very attribute she was trying to cultivate in herself. 'In many ways he was just what I was trying to be, detached without being cold, self-sufficient without being egotistic, sensitive but not vulnerable.' She was grateful for their friendship and happy to discover in the chief officer an unexpectedly sensitive side to which she could relate, a great benefit on the protracted journey ahead.

Frustrated by the ship's slow progress, Anna tried unsuccessfully to negotiate a passage on a ship sailing directly from Colon to South Africa but was prevented by the usual dispute over her passport credentials. So she stayed on *The Wanderer* and put out with a convoy of thirteen ships for Cuba, where a US torpedo boat came alongside with a caricature of Hitler painted in red and black on its side.

The convoy resumed its progress at the dilatory rate of seven knots, the escort ships acting as outriders as they laboured across the grey, shuffling Atlantic. It was six weeks since Anna had left Waitahanui, and the cold was starting to get to her. 'All I had left inside me below the brain', she wrote, 'was a small ball of northern cold and an uneven and rapid pulse.'

In January they arrived at New York in exhilaratingly glacial weather – a cold sun flashing across the glass fascias of skyscrapers and the air so raw that it hurt to breathe. Anna sat in the ship's bar drinking gin and vermouth, uncertain whether the passengers would be allowed ashore. When *The Wanderer* berthed, FBI officials came on board to fingerprint and photograph the passengers and crew. Anna was interrogated about her papers, profession and personal life before being cleared for landing. She attributed the implacable calm she had maintained under questioning to the newly adopted art of detachment she had been practising throughout the voyage, aware though she was at the same time of the fundamental defects in her method.

Finding herself in New York and taking the chief officer with her as a chaperon, Anna visited Charles Fuller at his apartment on 40 East 52nd Street, only to discover that despite his evident pleasure in seeing her again he had to leave town on business that evening for Pittsburgh, taking with him the familiar brown bag that Anna recognized from their travels. It was snowing big white eyelashes when Anna and the chief officer left Fuller's apartment, which he had given them for the night, and headed to the Viking Bar for drinks. Anna had shifted her dependency to alcohol, and given the constant references to it in 'The Cactus Sign' there is every reason to believe she drank steadily all day after noon.

The two returned to Fuller's apartment at 2 a.m. and slept together, Anna noted, without having sex, until the officer went back to the ship at 8 a.m., with the city under several feet of pristine blue snow. Anna stayed on in New York for three days by herself, visiting old friends and drinking whisky in all-night dives, until it was time for *The Wanderer* to take its place in the Atlantic convoy making the dangerous crossing to Britain. Anna wrote lyrically of her departure, at this mid-point in her life: 'I felt regret in my heart for the years and the dreams finished, the summers over, the days turning shorter, the heart beating colder in bitterness. That was a sad sort of feeling, but wonderful too.' They were part of a convoy of thirty ships, including an escort of six destroyers and six torpedo boats, travelling at a speed of about ten knots. The ship closest to hers was a whaler carrying tanks and planes. Everyone on board was ordered at all times to wear or carry their dark blue Ministry of Shipping lifebelts padded with kapok, and provided with whistles and torches. The convoy just ahead of them had been attacked intermittently for four days, and the captain was determined not to take risks.

They sailed into resolute cold in the Labrador Sea, the big freeze she encountered making a sufficiently lasting impression on Anna to resurface in the obdurately frozen landscapes of her novel *Ice*. In 'The Cactus Sign' she records the ship turning into a hallucinated artefact of blue ice.

The whole ship was coated in ice, the tanks and the water pipes froze so that there was no water for washing, even the cockroaches disappeared from the bar. The deck was a skating rink, thick fringes and swags of icicles hung from the rails, a monstrous white torch of ice flamed astoundingly from the mainmast, the thermometer stood permanently at about twenty below. It was like some movie of a polar ship. I couldn't stay out for more than a minute, it was too cold. If I touched anything on the way to my cabin at night in the black-out the skin burnt on my hand.

Confined below deck with inadequate light, Anna could not see sufficiently to read, write or make up. Time again seemed unreal, and the quirky, morose talk in the saloon centred on death and the ubiquitous atrocities of war. Everyone was supposed to sleep in their clothes in case of emergency and to keep a scram bag handy. Anna placed her papers, make-up, a sweater and a flask of brandy in hers, her rudiments of survival. Unable to sleep at night she drank sherry, brandy or gin at midday in the hope it would knock her out for the afternoon. Her days were mostly spent working on *My Soul in China* as a means of fictionalizing her recent past and of keeping a record of her voyage. Her only human contact comprised visits in the evening to the first officer's cabin, where they took it in turns to buy a bottle of liquor for the evening's consumption. The ascetically furnished bachelor's cabin without pictures or photographs became a refuge for Anna from the long solitary nights she so feared. Clinging to the rituals that helped her survive she recognized, 'The only thing to do was to get through the time and go on living: without going quite crazy, if possible.'

When the ship left Labrador the days grew perceptibly warmer and the pipes thawed out, but the convoy encountered spectacularly heavy seas, and *The Wanderer* was shipping water from the violent swell. They were chased by submarines, although safe from aerial attack on account of the turbulent weather. The whaler alongside *The Wanderer* was torpedoed and went under. Anna, gin in hand, went up on deck and with characteristic detachment watched a black spiralling column of smoke issuing from the whaler that had been split in two exactly amidships. Shaken by the incident and hardly able to believe in the reality of the events she was witnessing, Anna continued to write as the only means of making sense of her threatened existence. It was writing that allowed her to assert some degree of control over external events and fiction that interposed some sort of screen between her and the reality she so feared. Providing she could tell the story of what was happening in her own way, she could keep away from depression and the black hole that threatened to draw her in. She grew so accustomed to fear on her slow Atlantic crossing that she found it impossible to imagine living in any other state.

The world had simplified itself into a few unvarying fundamentals: motion, water, suspense, drinks, sleeplessness, insufficient light, talking to the first officer. These things seemed always to have been so, and I couldn't imagine that they would ever change.

As the weather picked up and grew warm *The Wanderer* entered the fast section of a convoy reorganized into two columns. The immediate danger to the ship now shifted from the threat of submarine activity to the fear of German pilots flying their Focke Wulfs out of the sun in sporadic opportunist raids.

When, after weeks at sea, Anna finally heard that the ship was due to berth within twenty-four hours she felt unequal to the terrifying prospect of facing life apart from *The Wanderer*. Inwardly, she had for a long time dreaded the voyage ending and had come to welcome being at sea, no matter the risk, as an alternative to the prospect of a reunion with her redoubtable mother in South Africa.

Her record of her wartime travels ends, as far as we know, with her eventual and hazardous return to England. She was already working on the stories published as *I Am Lazarus* by Jonathan Cape in 1945, and despite her inveterate state of nervous exhaustion she now faced another long-haul sea voyage to South Africa.

What seems apparent in this period of Anna's life is the psychological profile of a lonely, vulnerable woman, still attractive in her early forties, a marginal writer who had delivered the seminal *Asylum Piece* at a time unpropitious to publication, a person dependent on alcohol as a substitute for heroin and someone, above all, possessed of great courage and sustained by the conviction that she was a writer. She had cut free from the three principal men in her life, all of whom she had loved, and was resolved to be free. Her small income from writing and a diminished trust were supplemented by Charles Fuller's generosity – he continued to help her when she was in need for the next ten years – but essentially she faced an uncertain future alone.

The war in Europe, Russia and the East seemed to be ushering in the prelude to apocalypse that Anna's sensibility had long been anticipating. Given her nomadic life at the time and the uncertainty of survival, she instinctively chose the option of visiting her mother, whom she inwardly despised. This was not a matter of going home but an attempt to repair a relationship that had gone radically wrong. South Africa was neutral territory in terms of their emotional conflict, and with her mother married to a millionaire gay playboy who kept an entourage of houseboys in a sumptuous mansion in Monterey, in the Constantia suburb of Cape Town, Anna had reason to hope that a change of place would bring a shift in hostilities.

However, shortly after her arrival in South Africa in 1942 Anna received news that her son Bryan was missing in action, and in a state of deep trauma she was obliged to board ship back to England. In the face of this devastating loss she attempted suicide, and failing in that attempt she revived her pact with heroin.

9

Mutant Love

*

ANNA WAS FORTY-TWO when she first met Dr Karl Theodor Bluth in 1943, after the suicide attempt which led to her admission to the psychiatric ward at St Stephen's Hospital in London, where Bluth was working as a psychiatrist. She was treated by narcosis, and he was the first person she saw on her fuzzy, disorientated, drugged re-entry to consciousness. Twelve years her senior, he was a father figure who became her undisputed mentor, confidant and therapist until his death in 1964.

Bluth already had the beginnings of a heart condition at the time of meeting Anna. A letter he wrote her a number of years later from his Campden Street address gives a useful insight into the continuous depression he felt over symptoms that inhibited his work and creative lifestyle.

There is nothing but the mist of depression, every morning, if I wake up with pain; realising that I can't work, that I would overstrain myself in the attempt to enjoy life as before: and with it the fun of adventures, working, investigating and creating. I get terribly bored with my patients, and I dream of the time when I lived in some hospital, producing ideas, making my observations and stimulating other people. If I read the medical papers, everything I did 20 years ago turns up as a new idea with a tremendous circumstantialism. Everything is made academic and heavy. I have waited so long to go back into research; and now, after all restrictions upon my person have been lifted I find myself without health, strength or vitality. I think you are right: I should go to some special cardiologist and ask how to arrange the rest of my life. It will be no less and no more than several years; but if I spend it on trivialities and a praxis which tires me out, I waste whatever is left of me. There is no strength left in me, to fight for my very existence, and I have no securities: I'm terribly worried. I'm uprooted as well. If I do not fight for myself, I'll be finished . . . If I go to Sir John Parkinson, he will give the usual advice, to go slow, to rest; to look after my patients as a good stupid old ass; to reduce my metabolism, avoiding all sorts of thoughts, visions and adventures: what does he understand of my life? As for suicide I'm not ready: I'm afraid of leaving what I have done unfinished.

In a handwritten postscript to the typed letter, and as a clear reproach to Anna, who was away at the time in South Africa, he observed, 'But there is nobody who takes an interest in me', before going on to write of Anna's symptoms:

Your migraine may be due to hypoglycaemia – low blood sugar. Glucose should be helpful, also for the disturbance of vision. Dexedrine, Methedrine, Benzedrine, Ephedrine could be useful. Love KB.

Bluth was in fact to live another fourteen years after the crisis he outlined in his letter; but his overtly despondent state of mind, inflected with suicidal undertones, no doubt accentuated by a reference earlier in the letter to the possibility that Anna might not return to London, seems a lethal cocktail of dark energies to risk projecting on to someone who, despite being a friend, was also a patient regarded as an obsessive suicide. The role of therapist and patient were often, as in this instance, completely reversed, owing to the intimate friendship that had developed between them, and Bluth's extreme vulnerability – lack of money forced him to keep working, despite the obvious risk to his health – is evident in how he viewed his future as threatened by the possibilities of cardiac arrest.

Bluth and Kavan were both existentially isolated people whose fundamentally nihilistic views were none the less harnessed to the need to create from the imagination. Bluth's reference to the emotional void in his private life seems a pointer not only to Anna's notorious cool but also to an absence of concern on the part of his wife Theophilia. Nothing is known about either the research he did at Nottingham Central Hospital on first coming to Britain in 1936, or his work in London at St Stephen's Hospital and in private practice in Notting Hill Gate, so we have no knowledge of his professional working methods. What we do know is that Anna shared his conviction in the primacy of the individual's subjective reality as the only valid commentary on inner states, which conventional psychiatry oversimplified with its diagnoses of pathology. In a *Horizon* article,

'The Case of Bill Williams', a study Anna wrote about a psychological war casualty, she argues the case of the individual against the military.

Inevitably right from the start, the social machine is the enemy of the individual Bill Williams. It limits the avenues of his mind, it tips his feet and lays traps for his fingernails and his tongue. Every door closing, every form filled in, every official broadcast, every regulation, every propaganda slogan, is a munition in the war; Society versus Bill Williams.

This piece was published in June 1944, when Anna was working temporarily in a military psychiatric unit specializing in the psychological casualties of war. The subject allowed her to express her innate antipathy to institutions, political spin and any form of media-endorsed authoritarianism. Anna's lyrical defence of Bill Williams, in a written debate with the psychiatrist Dr Maxwell Jones and the psychoanalyst Dr Edward Glover over whether the state should be allowed to dictate to science the acceptable definition of normality, gave her the opportunity to champion the merits of the individual at the expense of totalitarianism.

Society does not want a man to live with a live flower inside him but to harden like mineral and live the life of a wheel. Yes, above all, the un-mortal, collective, prefabricated mechanism of society abhors the incalculable, the unique individual element, the unharnessed creative element, the flower which is apt to burst into flame and turn life into a blazing poem instead of an engineer's workshop. That flower at all costs it is determined to cut down stone dead.

This was written at the same time as Jean-Paul Sartre's *Being and Nothingness*, in which Sartre outlines the existentialist case for the absolute supremacy of subjectivity. Anna's affirmation of the individual threatened by the militaristic state affirms the Sartrean concept of phenomenology that is central to her work. She has erroneously been called a symbolist, but she would be more accurately described as the truest advocate of European existentialism in British fiction.

Ambiguously, she described her relationship with Bluth as 'a sort of love story', and it did indeed display the endless permutations of love that somehow contrive to work no matter the difficulties apparent in the relationship. It was not only that Bluth was married; Anna also met him on the rebound from her on–off affair with Charles Fuller. But Bluth offered her compassion and understanding rather than moral condemnation for the attempt she had made on her life; she found herself accepted intellectually, rather than relegated to the role of listener in male company, the part she had been expected to play in her two marriages as well as in her liaisons with Fuller and Hamilton.

Something of the indifference and cruelty Anna had experienced in her earlier admissions to clinics is powerfully re-created in the autobiographical reminiscence 'Some of the Things That Happen to Me'.

> They locked door in the clinic although claustrophobia. It doesn't matter if you scream or batter the furniture, there's nothing breakable in the room and anyway it's all been battered before by God knows how many desperate hands. It doesn't matter if your brains come out of your ears, it doesn't matter if you tear your heart out and eat it, it doesn't matter if you die fifty times over. Nobody cares, nobody takes any more notice than if you were a dog . . . What you get is to be kept in a warm bath for hours on end, to be strapped up in a sheet so that you can't move a muscle, to have a naked light shone in your eyes all night long.

This powerful indictment of mental health is entirely consistent with Anna's fiction, in which madness is perceived as less of a threat than the fear of confinement.

Anna claimed to have told her meeting with Bluth 'straight' in 'The Zebrastruck', from *Julia and the Bazooka*, which is our only source of information about the spontaneous, unsettlingly telepathic bond they shared right from the moment of their first encounter. Bluth attributed this to 'something to do with the cosmic rays coming from outer space. They strike some person or thing, and then you get a mutation like the stripes on a zebra.' Both were outsiders or aliens in the sense of not belonging to the world, and in their empathetic identification with the dispossessed and the mad as the carriers of the creative flame. They were according to Bluth 'mutants' – extraterrestrials whose method of bonding was far more durable than that achieved by ordinary human beings.

As a refugee doctor who worked inordinately hard in the interests of his patients, Bluth had come to neglect his first love, poetry, and it was the poet in him that Anna reawakened. Among her papers at the McFarlin Library at the University of Tulsa there are about a hundred poems that Bluth wrote and gave to Anna during the two decades of their inseparable friendship. For Anna, who was at heart a bruised romantic, the idea of encountering the one person totally sympathetic to herself, in a situation outwardly as antipathetic to forming personal relations as a hospital ward, was nothing less than miraculous. She wrote in 'The Zebra-struck':

> Their relationship had not been clearly defined. It had seemed to achieve itself spontaneously without effort on either side, and with no preliminary doubts or misunderstandings. To her it was both inevitable and invested with dreamlike wonder, that among all earth's teeming millions she should have met the one being complementary to herself. It was as if she'd always been lost and living in chaos, until this man had appeared like a magician and put everything right. The few brief flashes of happiness she had known before had always been against a permanent background of black isolation, a terrifying utter loneliness, the metaphysical horror of which she'd never been able to convey to any lover or psychiatrist. Now suddenly, miraculously, that terror had gone; she was no longer alone, and could only respond with boundless devotion to the miracle worker.

Anna's unusually euphoric response to meeting Bluth revitalized her as a person and a writer. Although she had published the transitional *Asylum Piece* in 1940 and *Change the Name* in 1941, before her felicitous meeting with Bluth, his encouragement helped push her imaginative faculty out on a longer reach. The intense subjectivity of *Sleep Has His House* (1948) and the more hallucinated fiction of *Eagles' Nest* (1957) and *A Bright Green Field* (1958) owe something of their author's confidence in experimenting with altered states in fiction to the imaginative dynamic that had become the natural dialogue between her and Bluth.

There is little doubt, too, that she took over his life and that her demands were met by his willingness to give her almost all his free time. In the stories she wrote after his death Anna recollected their mutual facility to access each other's minds.

> She was delighted to be included in his mysterious games, admitted to his world of imagination which no one else had been allowed to enter. As she gained confidence under his influence, he encouraged her to take an active part in the fantasies he invented, with which her elaborations merged indistinguishably, so that they seemed part of the original concept. She herself was surprised by the

closeness of their collaboration and the intimate interplay of their inventive-
ness, almost as if her brain had access to his.

('The Zebra-struck')

In the same story she recounts her first visit to Bluth's home at 53 Campden
Street, soon after leaving hospital, and how she was taken to an upstairs room in
which he saw patients and told to take off the attractive mustard-coloured silk
scarf splashed with black and crimson that she was wearing. Bluth had begun
unconventionally by lifting her fringe to explore her forehead, a gesture imply-
ing extraordinary familiarity on the part of a psychiatrist but in keeping with
their fluently instantaneous mutual attraction. He had then conducted her into
another room to assess her imaginative response to three hectically coloured and
imposing paintings that he kept on the wall – one of them a younger portrait of
himself, seated beside an emaciated female counterpart. Anna apparently
acquitted herself well with insightful responses, and as though she had been initiated into a ritual she began that day her long inner odyssey as Bluth's devoted
private patient.

Not that she was entirely uncritical of Bluth, finding in him an evasiveness
and a refusal ultimately to commit that kept her marginally defensive and at
times fazed by his unpredictability and the complex mind games he played. She
quickly learnt the art of being involved in intellectually heated discussions,
while at the same time taking care that she did not get herself burnt. As with
Charles Fuller, she found herself repeating a pattern of being involved with
someone on a deep level who had a prior commitment; this was a complex liaison
that allowed both parties unconditional freedom, while at the same time offering
something of the loyalty and trust implied by a relationship. It was an art at
which Anna had become adept.

They were both possessed of the rare capacity to live directly in the moment, to
the exclusion of past and future, and to maximize its effects. They took long walks
together through their neighbourhood and across the adjoining Holland Park and
Kensington Gardens, engaged in intellectual discussion; they visited exhibitions,
went to the theatre, and used wherever Anna was living as a safe place to meet.
Bluth saw them as two members of a future post-human species – two mutants
under the influence of 'the cosmic ray' – a speculation that Anna was prepared to
entertain for the sake of the relationship, and because she experienced the extraordinary chemistry that comes from discovering elective affinities.

They made no regular arrangements about meeting. When he was especially busy and absorbed in his work, he sometimes stayed away for days. It frequently happened then that, just when she felt she couldn't go on any longer without him, they would meet by chance, in the street, or at somebody's house, and the relationship which had been in abeyance would instantly be renewed with fresh ardour.

('The Zebra-struck')

Loving someone inevitably brings with it the increased awareness that the person will die, and for someone as sensitive as Anna the presentiment of Bluth's death, always there on account of his diseased heart, was the reverse side of the security she felt in his company. She admitted, too, that at times her possessiveness made her jealous even of his past and the people who were important to him, living or dead. This possessiveness was quickly translated into the irrational fear that he would abandon her suddenly, and it is easy to imagine the intense animosity she must have felt towards Mrs Bluth, a feeling that was entirely reciprocated.

Bluth was capricious, it seems, self-occupied rather than self-regarding, and put his work before Anna, relying on her need of him as he tested the boundaries of their relationship. He was unapologetic about his work taking precedence. Because of Mrs Bluth's suspicions, Anna's houses at 99 Peel Street and later at Hillsleigh Road became their regular meeting place. Bluth suffered his first heart attack two years after meeting Anna and for a period found it necessary to retreat from her, afraid that the sight of him ill and vulnerable would shatter her image of him, upon which she so greatly depended. When he did visit her again, in his capacity as a doctor coming to give her injections, all her worst anxieties were confirmed.

The sight of this pathetic, unsteady figure, instead of the swift catlike prowler she was expecting, came to her as a violent, agonizing shock. It was as if she had worn his image like a locket in her heart ever since their first meeting, and only now, this moment, saw how much he had altered since then. He looked so fragile and ravaged by illness that she was horrified and for the first few seconds wanted only to take him to some quiet place where he could rest and recover and she could make him smile.

('The Zebra-struck')

There is no admission from either Anna or Bluth that their relationship was ever consummated. Given Bluth's serious heart condition and Anna's increasingly asexual disposition, it would seem unlikely that sex intruded on the emotional complexity of a relationship in which the need for psychological support amounted almost to co-dependency. There was within Anna the romantic need to idealize a partner and to mythologize his qualities, and this she projected on to Bluth, who in turn wrote her hundreds of poems.

10

Critic at a Court of Queens

*

BACK IN ENGLAND from her extensive wartime itinerary and emotionally rejuvenated by the intense intellectual relationship she had formed with Dr Bluth, Anna found herself in need of supplementing the allowance she received from her mother, together with a small supplement from her stepfather Hugh Tevis. With this in mind, she worked in the capacity of secretary and editorial assistant to Cyril Connolly as editor of the highly influential *Horizon: A Journal of Literature and the Arts*, as well as becoming in the period 1944–6 one of the magazine's lead reviewers. *Horizon* quickly became an international platform for the leading Anglo-American and European artists and intellectuals of the 1940s. Gravitating naturally towards artistically disposed homosexual company, Anna made friendships with the likes of Peter Watson, who financed *Horizon*, Gerald Hamilton, who briefly became her lodger in the late 1950s, Michael Nelson and Denham Foutts.

The philanthropist and art collector Peter Watson was born in 1908 and educated at Eton and St John's College, Oxford. The Watson fortune, which made the family the sixth richest in Britain, was based on margarine. Peter was a thin, innately melancholic individual, who had a propensity for casual gay sex. Outrageous for the times, he drove an ostentatiously customized pink Rolls-Royce with fur seats and a jewel-encrusted dashboard. Because of his *élan* and fine-tuned aesthetic he was taken up by the likes of Cecil Beaton and Edith Sitwell. In the mid-1930s he moved to Paris, where he lived in a flat on the rue de Bac, assembling a priceless collection of the best modern paintings.

He shared his apartment with the young Florida-born Denham Foutts, whose mercenary nature led Christopher Isherwood to describe him as 'the most expensive male prostitute in the world'. In addition to his supremely handsome looks, Foutts was, like Anna, an incurable junkie; he demanded to be kept in style, and his previous roll-call of lovers had included Prince Paul of Greece. Foutts's drug of choice was cocaine, but like his self-destructive friend Brian Howard, who was also in Anna's circle, he smoked opium as well. Gore Vidal remembered him as being 'very pale, with dark lank Indian hair and blank dark eyes, usually half shut: he smoked opium and the light hurt his eyes'. 'The last of the professional tapettes', as Isherwood described Foutts, he resented Watson with the viciousness of a parasite. Like Anna he was dedicated to the constant reinvention of his own myth. He never confessed to his age; he retained a boyishly skinny figure, wore a black narrow-chested suit without shoulder-padding, a white shirt and black tie and had a lean face with an attractive Club Med permatan. Everything about his life appeared invented. He reputedly worked in his father's bakery in Florida until he was noticed and taken up by a passing cosmetics tycoon. According to his own account, he left the tycoon in Capri and became companion to a string of wealthy lovers. He helped solicit some of the contributions for *Horizon* and was given a large Picasso painting by Watson called 'Girl Reading'. Like Anna he travelled extensively in the war years and for a time lived in Los Angeles with Christopher Isherwood, who attempted to instruct him in the spiritual disciplines of yoga and meditation.

Perhaps because of his involvement with Denham Foutts, Watson liked to dress like an American and was an early advocate of wearing a belt instead of braces, as well as button-down collar shirts. An elegant, sensitive idealist subject to black pockets of depression – he was obsessed with death – his interests lay more with modern painting than with literature, but he proved to be the model patron for *Horizon*. He was immensely discreet in his generous patronage of individuals and understandably pro-gay in his selection of worthy causes. Anna, too, benefited privately from his anonymous beneficence. Apart from his loyalty to his hardcore gay entourage, because of an innate craving for perfection that left him invariably disillusioned Watson took people up and dropped them at an alarming rate. According to his close friend Stephen Spender, 'the best possible relationship with him was to be taken up by him very intensely for a few weeks, and then remain on his waiting-list for the rest of one's time'.

With Connolly as editor, *Horizon* initially set up office in the back room of Stephen Spender's flat in Lansdowne Terrace in Bloomsbury. The printer employed by the magazine was the 24-year-old Anthony Witherby, whose family firm H. and F. Witherby set the magazine's title in Elephant Bold Italic. They entered into a contractual agreement with Watson, who agreed to pay them £35 an issue to produce 1,000 copies at a published price of one shilling. Tom With-erby printed the first four issues of *Horizon*, but after he was called up the work on his recommendation went to Oliver Simon at the Curwen Press.

Connolly's editorial was suitably liberal and declared 'a policy of concen-trating on literary quality, both in well-known and unknown writers, and of disregarding both the feuds of the past and the inertia of the present in their effort to synthesise the aestheticism of the Twenties and the puritanism of the Thirties into something new and better'. It was also his intention to encourage 'such unpopular forms as the poem, the critical essay, the intimate journal, and the long short story'.

An early member of the *Horizon* staff, together with Anna, was Michael Nelson, an attractive young man who had been expelled from Bryanston and who formed a liaison with Watson. Years later Nelson published anonymously a *roman-à-clef* called *A Room in Chelsea Square*, a fictional account of the *Horizon* scene in which Watson, Connolly and Spender made caricature appearances.

Despite Connolly's resolutely apolitical stance and his belief in separating aesthetics from politics, *Horizon* maintained an anti-fascist stance throughout the war years, and Anna in her role as critic was inevitably drawn to integrate the discussion of politics into the psychological *motif* informing her wide-ranging literary reviews.

London was the scene of apocalypse in the early war years, and Connolly, Howard and Watson would all meet at Connolly's apartment at Athenaeum Court, a block of service flats off Piccadilly, as giant conflagrations raged across the city at night. Virginia Woolf, whose work Anna reviewed favourably, suffered structural damage to her flat in Mecklenburgh Square in Bloomsbury, while the *Horizon* office near by had to be shut down for several weeks after a ceiling sub-sided during one of the shatteringly destructive night raids. George Orwell, with whom Anna shared distinct affinities as a novelist, remembered

> sitting in Connolly's top-floor flat and watching the enormous fires beyond St Paul's, and the great plume of smoke from an oil drum somewhere down the river, and Hugh Slater sitting in the window and saying, 'It's just like Madrid – quite nostalgic.' The only person suitably impressed was Connolly, who took us up on the roof and, after gazing for some time at the fire, said, 'It's the end of capitalism. It's a judgement on us.' I didn't feel this to be so, but was chiefly struck by the size and beauty of the flames.

Although Watson financed the publication of the magazine, payments to contributors were small and, frustrated by lack of funds, Connolly announced in his editorial: 'We are unable to pay our contributors as much as we should like. If you particularly enjoy anything in *Horizon*, send the author a tip. Not more than one hundred pounds: that would be bad for his character. Not less than half-a-crown: that would be bad for yours.'

Anna's connections to the *Horizon* team provided her with a critical platform not only for assessing the merits and defects of her contemporaries but for showcasing her own deeply formulated ideas about the subjective novel. Her critical writing, reinforced by the study of psychology that Bluth had encouraged in her, was never confined to textual analysis or the simplistic breakdown of a book's structure but was also an exercise in self-discovery as a consequence of her reading. Like the art of psychobiography, in which the author personalizes his or her interaction with the subject, developing a transpersonal relationship in the process, Anna's criticism illuminated her working methods as much as those of the author under discussion. She was a profoundly intelligent, deeply sensitive reader of fiction and as uncompromisingly individual in her approach to others as she was in holding to the integral dynamic of her own highly experimental fiction. She was confident in her beliefs and had started with *Asylum Piece* to evolve a radically interiorized fiction, as is apparent in the facility with which she wrote about the modern novel in her *Horizon* reviews.

In the course of the two years in which she reviewed books for *Horizon* Anna took on the big names of her time, including Virginia Woolf, Rosamond Lehmann, Denton Welch, Alex Comfort, James Agee, L.P. Hartley, Henry Green, Ruthven Todd, Philip Toynbee and Aldous Huxley. Her review of *The Inquest* by Robert Neumann in the November 1944 issue expressed very clearly her advocacy of a novel informed by psychological rather than realistic tensions. Writing of the author's lack of inner attunement, she suggested:

He does not realise that characters come fully alive only through the elucidation of subconscious tensions which determine the basic patterns of human behaviour. A writer must speak, as it were, the language of the subconscious before he can produce his best work. And this is true, not only of such writers as Kafka and James Joyce, who communicate by means of a dream or fantasy medium, but also of those who describe the external happenings of the outer world. Even in stories of action employing a realistic technique, the source of genuine interest springs from an understanding of the fundamentals of personality. It is the interpretation of complexes, together with their sequence of inevitable events, which gives to any book the truly satisfactory rhythmic progression of music.

Here she was also describing the method she used for her richly textured novel of the late 1940s, *Sleep Has His House*.

Unafraid to venture into autobiographical anecdote as a means of preluding her review of Virginia Woolf's collection of short stories, *A Haunted House*, in the April 1944 edition, Anna employed a detail from her Burmese travels to stand as the central metaphor for her critique of Woolf's slightly skewed handling of the short story. As no other critic would have conceived of approaching their subject from so audaciously bizarre a tangent, it is worth quoting Anna's slightly parodic take on Woolf's aesthetic in full. The effects are hypnotic.

Among the sweet sellers at every Burmese *pwe* there used to be a man whose principal piece of apparatus was an inconspicuous little pipe. From this disarmingly simple object he would sooner or later start blowing into space a hairthin thread of spun sugar which, continually coiling and wreathing upon itself, would miraculously construct, first a web, then an ever-enlarging ball of indescribable light complexity, a vast sort of airy bolus, evolving improbably out of the slender pipe. That intricate and insubstantial creation, not to everybody's taste certainly, but floating with such an entrancing unearthly shimmer upon the air, seems to bear a semblance to the work of Virginia Woolf. There is the same fascinating elaboration of detail, threads laced and interwoven so subtly that their mazy ramifications have an air of fortuitness [*sic*], the same luminous lustre that never coarsens into transplendence or glitter, the same elusive charmed quality. The prosaic substance of everyday woven into the lovely, fragile mysteriousness of dream.

Whether one interprets this as an attempt to cue into Woolf's idiosyncrasies as a writer, or to upstage her, Anna was very sure that Woolf's gifts were unsuited to the short story. 'Virginia Woolf's peculiar genius does not find fullest expression in the form of the short story. The short story is like a small room in which is concentrated a brilliant light, unfavourable to the binding of elaborate spell.'

By the mid-1940s, and doubtless encouraged by Connolly, Watson and Bluth,

Anna had shifted from disinterest in the war to the promotion of ideological discussion in her reviews. Bluth's predicament as a refugee had alerted her to the reality of the death camps, and, more generally, to the disenfranchised, nomadic predicament of Europe's dispossessed. In discussing Woodrow Wyatt's reactionary anthology called *English Story*, she criticized the limitations of the selection caused by the failure of the contributors to address the question of re-visioning the state of the world and stressed the necessity to make a definitive break with the past by restructuring the future. She placed her trust in the individual as the unit of change, not the institutions of the state. Disgusted by the war machine and intolerant of propagandist autocrats and spin-doctors, Anna wrote powerfully of the need to dissociate from the ideological matrix generating military aggression.

What is needed is not a modified past, an indecent mechanical imitation of something dead, but a blazing new sun, a creation wholly and dynamically new. Reconstruction is useless: rejuvenation is useless: blood transfusions are no good at all. What is wanted is a new earth and a new man to inhabit the earth.

The purity of her vision was remarkable given that she was writing at a time in which the technological potential for brokering genocide had become an established fact. She was as impatient for political change as she was for a new literature, finding in the British sensibility an innate reactionary conservatism and a lack of originality that continues to this day to find its expression in the novel of one-dimensional social realism. The obstacle she encountered was the opposition that all British artists creating out of an imaginative dynamic continue to face, and that is the social constraint imposed on literature by the hegemony of moral restraint. If reportage is the accepted currency of British fiction, then Anna, criticizing that very trend in her review of an anthology of short stories called *The Windmill*, was quick to single out Henry Miller as the only revolutionary in the pack alive to the advantages of the psychological novel.

Miller, at any rate, is an author who is acutely aware of the possibilities and the importance of psychology in modern writing. One might also say that he exploits the psychological situation, as for instance, when he debunks psychoanalysis and presents it as the disease of those who make it their profession. It seems hardly fair to subject the rest of the contents of *The Windmill* to comparison with his enormous enthusiasm, beside which the style of most English authors is apt to appear either pedestrian or academic.

Anna's *Horizon* articles are immensely valuable in that they comprise the only defence of her literary aesthetic that she cared to publish. Launched on a career in which her novels were to have at best a cult readership, her solitary voice, increasingly marginalized and at the same time strengthened by the individuality that excluded her from the mainstream, remained free of all participation in the politics of literature and relied simply on the integrity of a tirelessly creative vision.

Even more than when she was berating the pedestrianism that she saw as the erosive agent in British fiction, Anna was most outspoken when expressing her fundamental sympathy with the humanistic ideals of the German Romantics. Clearly inspired by Bluth's enthusiasm for the likes of Novalis, Hölderlin and Schelling, when she reviewed *In Tyrannos*, a symposium of fifteen well-known German writers who had defected to England during the war years, Anna argued in favour of the intrepid individuality that had created freedom of intellectual thought in Germany. She maintained:

> it is impossible not to admire the tenacious idealism which for hundreds of years has maintained a continuous battle against aggression, preserving the flame of intellectual freedom which elsewhere succumbed to the stifling deadweight of Puritanism. For the astonishing fact emerges that Germany alone has kept alive the humanistic ideas which inspired the great men of the Renaissance period.

Intolerant as she was of authoritarianism and deeply suspicious of the motives of the collective, her instinctual antipathy to war surfaces as the topical undercurrent shaping her reviews. Using Harry Brown's war novel, *A Walk in the Sun*, as an opening to express some of her findings from working in a military psychiatric unit, she dismissed war as a 'pre-adult procedure' and its participants as having the mental age of fourteen. War to her was ultimately 'boring' in its negativity, its repetitive cycle contributing to escalating atrocities that, despite media documentation, no longer shocked. Anna rightly questioned the dangers implicit in becoming desensitized to horror in ways that ultimately sanction genocide. The influence of Bluth on Anna's thinking at this time is apparent in her elevated levels of political awareness and in her profound sympathy for Europe's refugees. Reviewing James Agee's *Let Us Now Praise Famous Men*, a study in words and pictures of three Alabama 'poor white' tenant families with photographs by Walker Evans, Anna was drawn to extracting the universal view from the particular. Shifting her focus to the predicament of refugees across the frontiers of a refashioned Europe, she wrote of this book:

> The problem raised is universal, not regional, and of the utmost urgency to all. It is a terrifying fact that the post-war world will be full of damaged and helpless human beings whose only fate, if any values are to survive, the whole human race must realize itself involved. Any representation, any experiment whatsoever, which may shock people into awareness of their responsibility to these undefended ones is of extreme importance. The ethical value of this book can hardly be exaggerated in that it tends, by disturbing the reader's emotional norm, to force upon him acknowledgement of his own profound implication in the matter.

Given the closeness of their intellectual discourse and the circles in which they moved at the time, it was not surprising that Dr Bluth should also be published by *Horizon*. Bluth's extended consideration of the German Romantic philosopher Schelling, in the September 1945 issue of the magazine, deserves attention not only as an illuminating enquiry into the archetypal basis of poetic imagination but also for the insights it provides into Bluth's mind as a psychiatrist. That Bluth conceived of creativity as a mystic process in which the artist dissolved his ego in the interests of reuniting himself with the psychological archetypes was not only consistent with his belief in the poet as inspired visionary but clearly central to his practice as a psychiatrist. Bluth saw imagination as the essentially depathologized drive-unit of the psyche and as a source not only of creativity but of reintegration. His advocacy of the use of drugs as an incentive to poetic vision is made clear by his discussion of opium in relation to the German Romantics. In Bluth's theory the Romantics in their search to regress to the primordial archetypes governing nature used psychoactive substances not only to disintegrate the ego but to enhance sensory experience. Opium was the most commonly used substance, the drug described by Carl Gustav Carus as the crystallized substance of the unconscious, able to carry a soul home to its dark origin. It was the spirit of night that Novalis found in the 'magic oil' of its brown juice. To these people opium was not a dangerous drug nor a symbol of delusion, but a draught of reality...

It was of course an opiate to which Anna was addicted and which Bluth so willingly prescribed. What interested Bluth about opium was the trance states the drug induced and the way the imagery it promoted rewrote reality for the user. For Bluth altered states reconnected the individual to his or her atavistic origins. The user

in this state could utter words of divine wisdom like the Delphic priestess who was hypnotized by narcotic fumes. Opium could induce a similar sleep in which the dreamer would remember his origins and look again, as Plato did, at the shape of living ideas. Schelling really put into practice a narcoanalysis of nature. If a mind could sleep deeply enough it could see the One – the 'identity' or the 'Absolute' as Plotinus recorded that he had done once or twice in his life.

Bluth's little-known essay on Schelling is a remarkable mini-synopsis of the psychological terrain with which he was familiar as both a poet and a medical practitioner. He doubtless discussed his meticulously considered piece with Anna in the course of writing it, as part of their shared intellectual dialogue.

Outwardly Anna had reason to be optimistic about her career as a writer. In 1945 she had short stories published in the *New Yorker* and *Harper's Bazaar*, and her second collection of stories *I Am Lazarus* was published by Jonathan Cape to critical acclaim. Doubleday in the USA published *Asylum Piece* and *I Am Lazarus* in one volume, focusing on the author's concern in both books with fictionalized experiences of mental breakdown. It seemed at the time as though Anna had at last created a niche for herself on both sides of the Atlantic as a writer concerned with conveying extreme psychological states in autobiographical fiction. Encouraging sales of the American edition also gained her some much-needed income, and Doubleday took out a contractual option on her next book, *Sleep Has His House* (1948).

She ceased reviewing for *Horizon* in 1946, at a time when the magazine shifted quarters from Lansdowne Terrace to two huge rooms at 53 Bedford

Square that Peter Watson had filled with Picassos from his Paris flat. Denham Foutts continued living a drug-wasted life in Paris. Watson, who toasted the change of office with a hundred bottles of champagne, had now taken up with the equally enigmatic Norman Fowler, an epileptic American who had served in the navy and whose recurrent seizures pointed towards severe psychological disturbance. When Watson drowned in the bath in mysterious circumstances in 1956 Fowler (who was the heir to most of Watson's estate) was present in the flat, and although the police recorded death by misadventure, given that Watson was perfectly healthy and neither drugged nor inebriated, his sudden demise was, to say the least, suspicious. In a letter to his friend Brian Howard, Watson had articulated the blues and feeling of becoming prematurely aged that were shared by the whole disillusioned *Horizon* group as it emerged from the ruins of war.

I seem to have suffered the death of feeling myself. I just can't react any more. It all seems so futile anyway, as we are under the sentence of death, I feel. If only the world contained some hope. Intelligence, freedom are monstrous luxuries which this world can no longer afford . . . It is paradoxical that those with least right to complain do complain but every day and in every way my sensibilities are attacked and outraged in London. What is maddening is that no one seems to notice as much as I do . . . How terrible it is to grow old. One loses so many tastes one had and seems to get no new ones at all. Wisdom doesn't settle anything – it only removes one from old friends and prevents one from making new ones. Then it is so humiliating to have all one's old beliefs and enthusiasms turned inside out. The only thing is to be young as it makes egotism elegant . . .

In November 1946 Anna underwent another course of detoxification, this time at the Sanatorium Bellevue in Kreuzlingen. She chose as a travelling companion Raymond Marriott's boyfriend, the valetudinarian George Bullock, a younger man who had also undergone psychiatric treatment and who idealized her almost to the point of emotional dependence. He took to sending her regular parcels of luxuries such as perfumed soaps and bath cubes, as well as gifts of flowers and strawberries. When she was unable to leave the clinic at Kreuzlingen, where she was undergoing narcosis, Bullock was trusted with the task of choosing the items of lingerie she required. His self-imposed role of factotum was rewarded by her writing: 'George Dear, I'm sorry to have caused you so much alarm and despondency over my pants – they are perfectly OK and the slip is exceptionally nice. I knew you had very good taste or I shouldn't have asked you to do the commission without detailed instructions.'

The two travelled together to Davros in second-class sleepers Anna had booked through Cooks, having secured a £60 advance from her publishers. They were sombrely photographed on a terrace, Anna looking morose in a floral shirt and smart slacks and George cowed into submission at her shoulder, wearing dark trousers, a tightly tapered jacket and shirt and tie. Both appear stiff and formally posed, as though the request to be photographed had been sprung on them, leaving them no chance to decline.

From Davros Anna travelled alone to the clinic at Kreuzlingen, where under the supervision of Bluth's friend Dr Ludwig Binswanger she made another partial attempt at detoxification. From the clinic Anna wrote to Bullock, 'I just want to say that I'm so glad we had this rather unusual chance of knowing each other. You say that I've helped you see things in a better perspective. If that's true, I am very pleased; for you have helped me in various ways – you have helped me, oddly enough, to make the decision about going to Busweigner [sic].'

A day later, partly missing George's attention and partly glad to be without it, she wrote uncertainly, 'How are you? When I say I hope and feel sure you're all right, I don't mean that I wouldn't like you to miss me – anyhow, just a little.'

The process of detoxification was not intended to clean the drug out of Anna's system altogether but was aimed at giving her a temporary respite from tolerance. In conformity with Bluth's policy of keeping Anna dependent rather than clinically depressed Binswanger administered the orthodox narcosis that Anna so dreaded and associated with temporary amnesia. 'The thing about Binswanger', she wrote to Raymond Marriott, 'is that he's far more rational and unprejudiced than any doctor except Bluth whom I've ever met. He quite agrees that my depressions are too hard to take without some alleviation.'

George Bullock's regular calls to the clinic punctuated Anna's intensely discomforting days and were a lifeline to her as she negotiated severe depression during reduction of the drug, confirming Bluth's unshakeable opinion that in her case heroin was required to alleviate an incipient pathology. 'It was nice to speak to you just now on the phone,' she wrote to Bullock in an undated letter. 'Just for a minute or two the horrible depression which hangs over me all the time seemed to move. But now it's back again – a great oppressive amorphous mass.'

Anna's profound understanding of psychological motives both in herself and in others made her friendships complex, and her tendency to analyse mutual dependencies is apparent in a letter she wrote Bullock from the clinic about his acute inferiority complex, which was invariably exaggerated in her company. After having made clear her belief that they were both unconsciously in search of a 'parent-substitute', she addressed the unequal nature of their friendship.

> I don't believe there's any reason for you to fear damage from me, so that this
> anxiety to protect yourself in advance seems to indicate the existence of some
> deep-rooted complex which it would certainly be unwise to disturb. Your dread
> of being put into an inferior position will disappear, I feel sure, as soon as you
> realise that inferiority and superiority are not concrete objects like chessmen,
> but only concepts inside your head. I suppose life can be turned into a kind of
> chess game played for points, but that seems a very limited way of living.

She had obtained a sum of money from her family to help extend her conva-lescence in Switzerland, and she offered to pay for Bullock to come out and join her as a secretary and companion, but complications with a pulmonary relapse caused by a shrivelled lung prevented him taking up her generous offer. At the time Bluth was advising on Bullock's precarious health, and Anna was quick to reassure George of his progress. 'I expect Bauer told you he had a talk with Dr Bluth about you on the phone. Bluth suggested giving you some vitamins etc., but Bauer didn't think it necessary as he said you were making a good recovery and there was nothing to worry about.'

Informed of Anna's descent into chronic depression caused by narcosis, Dr Bluth managed to overcome various bureaucratic and marital restraints to join her in Kreuzlingen, for what was on his part a rare holiday, despite the insistent demands made on him by Anna's dysphoric state.

Anna returned for the summer of 1947 to her flat at the White House in Ken-sington, a property once owned by Whistler, and busied herself with revising *Sleep Has His House* for publication by Cassell's, before once again sailing for South Africa in October in the hope of receiving a restorative familial boost to her low morale. The story of the middle-aged writer returning home oppressed by an overwhelming sense of failure for which there is no readily available remedy is a familiar one. Risking your life for a vision that plays no part in the context of everyday reality – and wearing the consequent scars of financial insecurity, depression and acute alienation – is an uncomfortable state. Living in a gold room with a rococo gold four-poster bed, Anna felt frozen into a vacuum-sealed mausoleum by the relentless ennui of domestic routine at the Tevis mansion, where empty gestures and superficiality substituted for authentic emotion. Writing to Raymond Marriott, Anna complained of the meaningless round of daily functions. 'Staying with my mother is rather frightful of course . . . this sort of pointless luxury somehow contrives to make itself into a tyrannical machine, so that one is caught up in a perpetual round of drinks, changing one's clothes and so on, and is never able to do anything one really wants to.' She was also irritated by her mother's obsession with having a footman follow her at all times, plumping up cushions that she had flattened and restoring anything she had touched to its proper place. Anna felt dehumanized by 'the smooth impersonal planning of a perfectly equipped household where money is no object'. She was additionally depressed in February of the following year by the bad reviews given *Sleep Has His House* and the book's commercial failure.

There was also the problem of drugs and the obsessive fear that she would run out, although with her usual underworld instincts Anna seems to have found a regular source in South Africa, informing Marriott, 'It will certainly be impossible to cope with the situation here without the usual paraphernalia – much easier to obtain here, by the way.' Only by staying in her own altered reality could she tolerate a mother who was rooted so deeply in her psyche as to be a source of continuous disturbance. Writing letters was Anna's only recourse as she struggled with her mother's negative influence; she told Marriott of her very real fear of being reduced to paralysis by being too long around her mother.

> I'm really terrified in a childish nightmare way of getting stuck out here, unable to move, and petrified forever in a repetition of my childhood isolation. It must be bad for me psychologically to stay so long in the neighbourhood of my mother. All the old frustration paralysis feeling comes over me. I feel less and less able to work or have any independent existence – less and less a real person.

Hugh Tevis made a concerted attempt at matchmaking, introducing Anna to Cass Canfield, a wealthy New York publisher. Together the pair visited Great Karoo, but Anna adroitly succeeded in making Canfield into a friend and blocked any attempt at a more serious relationship.

Sleep Has His House was Anna's most experimental book to date. The title was lifted from a passage in John Gower's *Ceyx and Alcyone*. Anna took the method first developed in *Asylum Piece* a stage further, advancing the case for a strictly subjective, nocturnally themed poetic novel. Written in what she termed 'night-time language', the book explores a dream topology in which reality disintegrates into a series of hallucinated fractal entities. Way ahead of its time, in its slowed-down, high-resolution enquiry into the appearance of things, the book was clearly shaped by Anna's harrowingly traumatic attempts at drug withdrawal. Fusing the influence of Kafka's totalitarian world of bureaucratic automata with her own belief that 'every single possibility or impossibility is true somewhere to someone at some time', the upended, brilliantly morphed and surreal landscapes of *Sleep Has His House* pushed her stylistic exploration to its limit.

Pre-dating Alain Robbe-Grillet and the episodic nature of the *nouveau roman*, in which detailed description takes precedence over narrative development, *Sleep Has His House* came a decade too early to help advance Anna's career. It directed a superabundance of free-floating hypnogogic imagery into the verbal equivalent of film-loops – the visual quality of the writing is never less than stunning – but the method proved unpopular with reviewers and the book was a commercial failure. The merging of dreamlike landscapes with reality throughout the fragmented text succeeds in exploring a method that in time would lead to the shattering of apocalypse in *Ice*. Nothing in the book is forgettable; for instance:

> A hard judge-like man of about sixty-five, personifying the more hidebound and sadistic type of disciplinarian, woodenly placing his feet in bright patent leather shoes. Simpering over his stiffly encircling arm, a horribly travestied sweet young girl of sixteen in perfectly transparent white muslin; the rouged points of her breasts stand out through the white like the red spot on a tarantula.

The bad reviews came at a time when she seemed at last to be gaining some reputation as a writer. She found them profoundly disillusioning and they temporarily extinguished her creative energies. She wrote to Raymond Marriott,

> For the first time in my life I am unable to work, and wonder if my career as a writer is over. For years I've depended on my work as a *raison d'être*, but now that seems to have gone down the drain . . . One thing is certain, I shall have to figure out something, for it is clear I shall never be a success at writing now.

She returned to London on 10 March 1948, again taking a flat at the White House in Kensington as a temporary base, and she offered it as a refuge to George Bullock when she returned to Kreuzlingen in May, alarmed by her susceptibility to infection from needles and again heavily habituated. She wrote to Rhys Davies on 26 May of the seriousness of her condition. 'I've been laid low since the day I got here with a form of acute septicaemia: high temperature, huge and loathsome abscesses which had to be cut open under an anaesthetic and drained with innumerable tubes. I feel rather like Job.'

She stayed on at the clinic for two months. Crushed by her disappointment with both the production and the critical reception given *Sleep Has His House*, she wrote to Cassell's asking them to release her from her contract. Something of the camp tenor of her friendship with Rhys Davies is sounded in another, more playful letter written from the clinic. 'What romantic ideas you're getting, all mixed up with the respectable green cabbages of the Edgware Road – fanning people with white ostrich feathers indeed! Though I could certainly do with a fan of some sort (preferably electrical) as it's suddenly turned fearfully hot here.'

She spent the rest of 1948 in London, and in anticipation of making what was to be her final voyage to South Africa in February 1949 she underwent another period of detoxification, this time in a London clinic, the Greenway Nursing Home. Her depression had returned with a vengeance, as she described to the overly solicitous George Bullock: 'I can't write or even speak to anyone because I feel too depressed . . . For the last few days I've just been existing inertly like a limpet on a rock.'

She recovered sufficiently to travel and made a sometimes violently turbulent crossing to South Africa, where she stayed from mid-February to May 1949. Bored, disorientated and feeling disaffected with the neurotically punctilious routine, she asked Rhys Davies to send her copies of *New Writing* and the *New Statesman*. In return she sent Rhys a parcel containing items he could not procure in London: '2? lb tin of ham, veal loaf, tongue, peaches, mixed fruit for cakes, etc. No peanut butter.'

She returned to London in a state of crisis. Her allowance had never been increased, and except for a small edition produced in collaboration with Bluth, published by Gaberbocchus Press in 1949, she did not publish another book for seven years. In 1956 she self-published five hundred copies of *A Scarcity of Love* through the Southport publisher Angus Downie, who unfortunately went bankrupt almost immediately after the book appeared.

Despite her disappointment over the poor reception given *Sleep Has His House* Anna always managed eventually to summon enough conviction in her own talent to sustain her through personal crises. Her sort of writing was never going to be popular, and she was realistic about the prospects, as she wrote to Raymond Marriott: 'As so-called literature becomes more and more commercialised, "real" writing is bound to take more and more obscure and personal forms until it's finally only intelligible to a small number of sensitive people.'

11

Dr Bluth and the Mad Business

*

I N *The Sun at Midnight*, a notebook that
the British poet David Gascoyne kept during his incarceration at Horton mental
hospital in Surrey in the late 1960s, Gascoyne made the following entry under
Confidential Pharmaceutical Information:

> During the early years of what I now know I can only call my vocation, I dis-
> covered the special properties of the amphetamine compounds. This was during
> the War, when amphetamine preparations were freely available at all chemist
> shops (of which a large number are familiar to me). I was for a short period
> under the control of a refugee I will refer to as K.T.B., but dangerously
> exceeded his prescribed doses, and under the influence of the drug once found
> myself on Christmas Eve at the gates of Buckingham Palace, believing I had a
> great spiritual message to deliver.

Gascoyne told me that on the day he set off for Buckingham Palace, bringing
with him news of imminent apocalypse, he had been injected by Dr Bluth with a
cocktail of amphetamine, bull's blood and B vitamins. 'The mental disturbance
leading up to this could be described as resulting from an advanced form of
chiliasm. This took the form of an overwhelming conviction that the end of the
world as we know it was at hand.'

In an unpublished journal entry Gascoyne also remembered Dr Bluth ham-
mering on a white piano in his Notting Hill surgery before injecting him with a
mixture of ox blood and methadone and that Anna Kavan and Conrad Veidt
were beneficiaries of the same treatment.

Anna's confidential case notes, if indeed Dr Bluth kept any, have disappeared
along with most of her private papers. No proper diagnosis of her state has ever

been given, and yet her symptoms were sufficiently distressing to keep her in and out of psychoanalytic consultation for much of her adult life and to cause a number of severe breakdowns requiring hospitalization. Certainly her case cannot be given the taxonomy of a specific pathology. The geography of psychological distress explored in her novels and the dissociative states common to nearly all her characters suggests that like most highly imaginative artists she had psychotic experiences without being generically psychotic. While biomedical models of madness have largely been deconstructed in new approaches to mental health and replaced by symptom dimensions, Anna's hallucinated reality gravitates in its disturbance towards psychosis-proneness, or at least the experience of psychotic phenomena. There is of course a distinction between biochemical hallucination and the dysfunctional neurotransmission that may be its cause, and the experience of psychotic phenomena in which the person is witness to disturbing visual imagery but sufficiently detached not to take it for reality. It is my belief that people with strong imagination produce some kind of endogenous hallucinogenic substance that contributes chemically to opening out visionary pathways of the kind found in Anna's work. It is what distinguishes imaginative work from its counterpart, social realism, and it is also what makes people afraid of the art of those who express themselves through continuously altered states. To those who fear it in themselves, madness is taboo.

Beginning with *Asylum Piece* in 1940, and continuing through the fictional studies of madness in *I Am Lazarus* (1945), Anna prefigured by almost a decade the confessional preoccupation with madness that entered literature in the late 1950s with the publication of Robert Lowell's hugely influential *Life Studies* (1959), the book which contributed most to making breakdown a legitimate subject for literature. Lowell's willingness to go public about his periods of confinement and the mania that disrupted his life was taken up in rapid succession by the likes of Sylvia Plath, Anne Sexton and Angela Carter, but it is Anna who deserves to be credited for writing about madness and being hospitalized at a time when to do so invited both controversy and suspicion.

Rhys Davies tells us that Anna suffered from periods of black depression for which she took amphetamines, although she may also have used them to fire herself from the effects of heroin. There is little doubt that her continuity was constantly threatened by a sense of catastrophe that invaded the boundaries of her personality. Heroin and a depressive mode may well have been her way of blanking it out or learning to tolerate the fear of personal shattering.

Anna's inseparable friend and private psychiatrist Dr Karl Theodor Bluth was born on 5 May 1892 in Berlin. He studied literature and philosophy in Bonn, Berlin and Jena and received his doctorate in 1914. As a young man he started out with literary ambitions and published a first volume of poetry, which reveals stylistic affinities with the late Expressionists, in 1918. In the early 1920s he wrote plays, before working in a psychiatric hospital in Bavaria in 1923–4. After his return to Berlin the 1930 staging of his play *Die Emporung des Lucius* (written in 1924 and aimed against totalitarian systems of government) was banned after a short run. He resumed his studies and received his doctorate in medicine in Berlin in 1934 for a dissertation on the poet Novalis, *Medizingeschichtlies bei Novalis*. As one of the writers whose books were condemned and burnt by the National Socialists and whose prescient political radar picked up on the rapidly escalating momentum of Nazism, Bluth providentially escaped Germany for Latin America in 1934. In 1936 he came to Britain, and after a period spent at Nottingham Central Hospital he went to live in London and established a medical practice at 53 Campden Street in Kensington.

As a psychiatrist Bluth appears to have been a maverick who discouraged diagnostic labelling and who looked to creativity as the means of liberation from psychologically extreme states. He attracted writers and artists to his practice, including David Gascoyne, George Barker, Julian Trevelyan, Peter Watson and Cyril Connolly as well as Anna Kavan. When George Barker consulted Bluth it was because he continually heard peacocks screaming in his head. Bluth told him that he was a 'religious maniac' and prescribed Methedrine for the condition, a stimulant that had recently been developed to keep pilots awake during long-range bombing raids but used initially in psychiatry to correct a variety of mental conditions. In David Gascoyne's case it was the audiovisual hallucinations accompanying schizophrenia that took him to Bluth, symptoms that Gascoyne described as like having a radio turned on in his head, the stereo panning inter-hemispherically. A bohemian poet dressed ubiquitously in a pinstripe suit and arty tie, worn to identify himself as a gentleman should he attract attention by freaking out in public – Gascoyne knew both Anna and her unconventional consort Dr Bluth in the 1940s.

Bluth's early years as a trainee psychiatrist were dominated by Freudian studies and what has come to be known as the Kraepelin paradigm, the arbitrary classification of stress symptoms into diagnostic clusters as the main organizing principle for psychiatric practice and research. With disastrous consequences for psychiatry Kraepelin grouped classifications such as catatonia, hebephrenia and dementia paranoides into an illness he called dementia praecox, which would become the most widely abused concept in psychiatry. Any deviation from the Kraepelin rule of linking diagnosis to a specific treatment carried serious implications, and to Bluth, who was chiefly interested in the creative aspects of madness, the framework imposed damaging limitations not only on the variants of individual expression but on the boundaries of imagination itself. It should be remembered that the young André Breton began life as a junior psychiatrist working with French soldiers traumatized by shell shock and that it was through witnessing their free-associated images in this state that he struck on the idea of surrealist experimentation with automatic writing. Working with his collaborator Philippe Soupault, he produced an automatic text that became *The Magnetic Fields* (1919).

Like Breton, Bluth was a poet who looked to psychiatry not only as a means of liberating madness from pathology but of finding in its arena some overlap with the creative experience. Bluth chose to write his medical doctorate on the poet Novalis, who is best known for the quintessential romanticism inherent in his mystic sequence of poems *Hymns to the Night*. Novalis was inspired to write these after having a vision while visiting the grave of his young wife Sophie von Kuhn, whom he had secretly married when she was still only thirteen. Novalis, who was to die of consumption at the age of twenty-nine in March 1801, was, like his contemporary Hölderlin, subject to periods of breakdown, although the latter's condition was much more severe and led to hospitalization.

Novalis in his grief succeeded through obsession in repeatedly visualizing the dead Sophie and continued to treat her as real. In a journal entry he wrote: 'In the evening I went to see Sophie. Moments of overwhelming enthusiasm. With one breath I dispersed the tomb like a heap of dust – centuries seemed no more than instants – her presence became evident to me – I had the feeling she was on the point of appearing.'

Bluth's attraction to Novalis was not solely as a psychobiological case study, for it contained a tangent of occultism in its undertow. Novalis studied kabbala, magnetism, mineralogy and the occult sciences, some of his more arcane beliefs finding expression in the posthumously published collection of prose fragments called *Pollen*.

In the course of her early attempts to kick the heroin habit Anna was subjected to narcosis or deep-sleep therapy with the aid of barbiturates such as Somnifen and later to insulin-coma therapy, treatments she grew to loathe for the feeling of partial disconnection from reality that they created. The patient undergoing narcosis received an increased daily dose of insulin to induce sleep, then coma, followed by a state of deep unconsciousness. The patient was monitored and permitted to spend no more than twenty minutes in coma before being brought round with a strong glucose solution administered through a rubber tube in the nose. Insulin coma doubled the proportion of recoveries from schizophrenic symptoms at the Maudsley Hospital in London but failed long term for Anna in her various attempts at detoxification in Swiss and London clinics.

Other major developments in psychiatry during Dr Bluth's London residency included the post-war popularity of therapeutic communities. The Tavistock Clinic in London was the first, founded in 1920 by Hugh Crichton-Miller and John Rawlings as an out-patient service with a strong psychoanalytic orientation for patients with nervous illnesses. Others followed, including the Social Psychiatry Centre established by Joshua Bierer in 1946 in two war-damaged houses in Hampstead. From this successful start Bierer and his colleagues drew up the template for a possible day hospital that would combine a patients' social club with psychodrama, group psychotherapy, electro-convulsive therapy and insulin cure. The idea of the day hospital was to shift the focus away from clinical diagnosis and to offer considerably more humane care than was provided by traditional institutions.

In terms of toxic or biological psychiatry, the efficacy of LSD to induce psychosis experimentally had been discovered in 1943, and although Anna admitted to having taken LSD recreationally we have no knowledge of Dr Bluth being the source of the drug. It was the anti-psychiatrist R.D. Laing who, attracted to the psychotomimetic properties of LSD, used the drug both on himself and on his patients to explore schizophrenia. From David Gascoyne's experience with an unorthodox cocktail of vitamins and drugs it would seem that Bluth experimented with psychopharmacology according to his perception of the individual's needs.

With respect to the interpersonal relationship between analyst and patient, it is interesting to read Anna's appraisal of Bluth from the dual viewpoint of close friend and patient. Writing to her friend George Bullock in 1947, she assessed his personality:

> With regard to Bluth's attitude – one would have to write a psychological treatise to explain it. I think I understand his behaviour, but not the underlying cause of

it. It's not that he objects to the idea of my going away – theoretically I believe he wants me to go – as I told you. But there is something in himself that preoccupies him to the exclusion of everything else. It's this preoccupation that on occasions cuts him off from reality and makes his conduct seem inexplicable and contradictory. He has been ill during the last week or so, and of course that increases the tension. I suppose I've been more intimate with him than other people during the two years I've known him, so that I'm bound to be the target for aggressive manifestations that always attack those who are closest and most vulnerable. The dual friend–patient relationship is inevitably hard to maintain and liable to misunderstanding. An additional difficulty is the hostility felt by Theo [Bluth's wife] towards me. She dislikes me intensely and is constantly trying, consciously or unconsciously, to make trouble.

Bluth's therapeutic relationship with Anna was anomalous, observing none of the boundaries normally maintained between therapist and patient, especially the rule that the therapist should refrain from letting his personal life intrude on a space that is exclusively the patient's. Bluth committed the cardinal error of becoming Anna's closest friend and losing his professional distance from her in the process. They saw each other most days, and after Anna's return to London in 1948 they collaborated on an Orwellian animal fable, with undertones of apocalyptic catastrophe, called *The Horse's Tale*, an experimental novel not without literary merit.

The original edition of *The Horse's Tale* was limited to three hundred copies, most of them given away to friends, so this book has remained an unknown curiosity to Anna's cult readership. This short allegorical novel, with its sense of impending catastrophe and nuclear flame-out, characteristic of Anna's vision of landscapes radically altered by military intervention, begins on a note of devastation that anticipates the disaster sites mapped out in the post-apocalyptic terrain of *Ice*.

That was a bad time for us horses: we used to stand around with empty faces, unsheltered, unfed; we were nobody's business. Foreigners had invaded the country, won all the battles, killed off all the fighting men, raped the women, taken prisoner the king himself. Houses and whole villages were on fire: wherever you looked you saw smoke rising into the sky.

Bluth's contributions to the book are evident in the existential psychology applied to Kathbar, the book's equine protagonist, a circus horse who has a way with poetry and is susceptible to Anna's *bête noire* – depression. When Kathbar hits bottom,

> Still another doctor, a psychiatrist this time, was called in . . . After a long talk he informed me that I was severely depressed, though whether it was an endogenous or a reactionary depression, he could not say without further investigation. He also said that I had been overworking.

Bluth's attempts to declassify the arbitrary grouping of symptoms under a diagnostic name are powerfully taken up in Kathbar's denigration of the psychiatric model as both useless and inflexible.

> I felt at the same time despairing and cross. What was the sense of paying so much money and listening to so many words just to hear at the finish what one knew to begin with? I told him that I had certainly been under a terrible strain on account of my work, a strain that he, as a man working mechanically according to textbook rules, couldn't possibly understand. The psychiatrist was offended by this implication that his profession needed no creative gift. Turning his back on me angrily, he told the painter in malicious tone that I was a psychopath, unbalanced, autistic and somewhat degenerate. He wondered whether I was an alcoholic, or addicted to any drug? There was nothing he could do for me, anyhow, either in the way of analysis or psychotherapy. He advised a prolonged rest; preferably in some closed establishment.

I take this passage to have been written by Bluth as a lacerating excoriation of textbook psychiatry, although it could equally be Anna making an undercover attack on her past experience of the analyst's couch. Either way the sentiments expressed anticipate the similarly iconoclastic dissatisfaction with orthodox psychiatry expressed by the dissenting anti-psychiatrists Thomas Stasz and R.D. Laing a decade later.

Anna was mostly negligent in paying for Bluth's professional services, a lapse accountable to the blurring of distinctions in their relationship. The outstanding bill was eventually paid by her wealthy stepfather Hugh Tevis, much to the chagrin of Mrs Bluth who had little but contempt for Anna's capriciously bohemian and impractical lifestyle. Admonitory letters sent by Theo Bluth demanding payment for her husband's home visits and consultations usually met with a blank on Anna's part. In 1949, with bills outstanding over a long period for the doctor's professional services, Theophilia Bluth was forced to write to Mrs Tevis in South Africa about Anna's persistent negligence. Her letter is interesting for the details it provides about Anna's professional treatment.

> I wonder whether you would be kind enough to pay some attention to the fact that your daughter Miss Kavan has been unable to pay off her debts to my husband. She paid several instalments, and the last one in April '49, and has ceased to pay any instalments ever since. When your daughter was under my husband's care, she assured me that she would settle the matter 'as soon as she would not be so hard up'. And in the late summer 1944 Captain Maberley (on your behalf) insisted on my husband's continuing his treatment, although Dr Bluth had suggested that the care should be passed on to Dr Harris. The facts are confirmed by two letters from Captain M (the 2nd and 26th September 1944) and known both to Dr Harris and Dr Scott, who had assured Dr Bluth that his fees would be paid by the patient's family. So I wonder whether you would ask one of your advisers to look after the matter and settle it in a friendly way.
>
> Miss Kavan was a case of obsessional suicide. After several revivals she had to be watched very carefully; for periods she had to be seen several times every day. Several withdrawals were given, continuous narcosis and psychoanalysis, and once Dr Bluth was called upon to see the patient urgently in Dr Binswanger's asylum in Switzerland. You will understand that Dr Bluth feels hurt, if these facts are ignored, if he is not paid for his work, if letters he wrote to the patient's family are not answered. Nevertheless, in January '48 he had to help the patient again; he got in touch with the patient's present doctor and Dr Backus. Some of the doctors have suggested that for some psycho-pathological reasons Miss Kavan would not pay her fees, even if she were in a position to do so. She probably would feel that I myself and my husband, who has given her valuable support, were no longer friendly disposed towards her. For this reason I have been extremely reluctant to deal with the case in a routine way.

Given the nature of their mutually dependent friendship, and the amount of time her husband spent at Anna's house, their holidays together and their forming a couple at parties, Theo Bluth had every reason to feel neglected at Anna's

Anna Kavan's icy blue eyes are a prominent
feature in this later gouache and watercolour
self-portrait on paper (343 mm × 242 mm).

Helen Ferguson as a tentative
brunette, *c.* 1914

In Burma, *c.* 1921

Helen's son Bryan Ferguson with
Ann Latch, *c.* 1930

Helen with her second husband
Stuart Edmonds, c. 1932

Helen, by now known as Anna Kavan, and Dr Karl Theodore Bluth in
Kreuzlingen, Switzerland, 1947

Anna with her friend the art collector
and philanthropist Peter Watson in
Kreuzlingen, 1947

A rare meeting for Anna with her
mother in South Africa, 1947

Anna with her friend and admirer
George Bullock in Davos,
Switzerland, 1947

An intense, closely cropped self-portrait in oils (388 mm × 292 mm)

The volcanic landscapes around Waitahanui, New Zealand (above), and the frozen wastes of the Labrador Sea (left) are recalled in this mixed media work on paper (242 mm × 343 mm and 343 mm × 242 mm). They seem also to have informed the encroaching, desolate terrain of the novel *Ice*.

Reflections and invented
lives. Mixed media on paper
(496 mm × 343 mm)

The gilded harp was inherited
from Anna's mother and displayed
at both the Peel Street and
Hillsleigh Road residences.

Anna's later homes. Left: 99 Peel
Street, a quiet turning off
Kensington Church Street, London
Below: 19 Hillsleigh Road off nearby
Holland Park Avenue

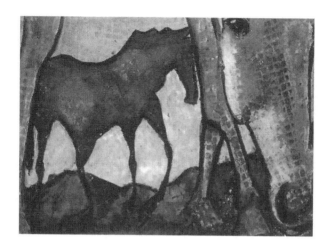

One of Anna's experiments with her 'mosaic' technique; gouache on paper (356 mm × 496 mm)

A gouache and watercolour landscape study on paper (348 mm × 496 mm)

Dancing swans in gouache and watercolour on paper (254 mm × 311 mm)

An atmospheric depiction of a nighttime prowl; gouache and watercolour on paper (210 mm × 159 mm)

This late portrait, androgynous and atrophied, suggests terminal addiction through the deeply cratered eyes; gouache and watercolour on paper (343 mm × 242 mm)

Who are you?: The many layers of Anna's personality, separating her from the outside world; pen, ink and chalk on coloured paper (330 mm × 292 mm)

In many of Anna Kavan's
drawings and paintings,
forms collide and images
metamorphose into
hallucinogenic visions as in
the dream-inspired works of
the earlier Surrealists
(483 mm × 343 mm, 483 mm
× 343 mm and 496 mm ×
343 mm)

Victim of a murderous sexual act? Gouache on board (224 mm
× 267 mm)

An intense 'mosaic' portrait of
Dr Bluth; gouache on paper
(343 mm × 247 mm)

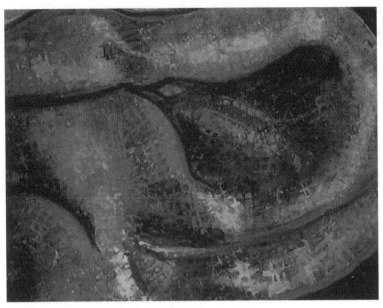

A near-abstract work depicting a naked torso; gouache on paper
(343 mm × 496 mm)

Acrobatic block-like figures
painted with an upbeat Fauvist
palette; mixed media on paper
(496 mm × 343 mm)

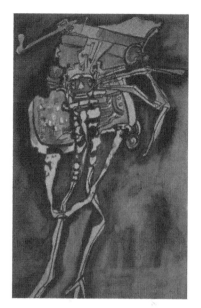

Top left: Fish rise in dumb passivity
towards an angler's worm. Gouache
and watercolour on paper (343 mm ×
242 mm).

Top right: A skeletal figure appears
to alternate between emaciated clown
and cybernautic warrior. Gouache,
watercolour and pen on board
(488 mm × 343 mm).

Left: A pallid angel that could be
the glass girl in *Ice*, an elusive almost
incorporeal figure pursued for her
sexual allure. Gouache, pen and ink
on board (242 mm × 196 mm)

Mixed media work, possibly produced as an illustration to the short story 'A Visit', from *Julia and the Bazooka*, written in 1965 (242 mm × 350 mm)

Lounge lizard on leopard skin: Anna Kavan at home at the time of the publication of *Ice*, in 1967

expense. There was also understandable resentment on Mrs Bluth's part at the regular calls for nocturnal visits, caused by Anna's panic attacks and her need for reassurance, that were an additional strain on her husband's time.

There are artists who work so far out on the edge that their mental health is constantly under threat. Whether in these instances creativity is the poison or the cure is open to endless debate. As a writer inhabiting a hallucinated neural precinct and one who felt constantly threatened by the social order and the recklessness of ideological destiny, Anna wrote to give her fragile identity a place in the world. Words were her DNA sequencing and imagery their transcription. As long as she was working on the page and re-creating the universe in ways that were acceptable to her, Anna could bring control to the inner traffic of disturbance she so feared. Her empowerment came through writing, although outwardly it made nothing happen. Writing, too, was a means of getting a lift out of depression. Dr Bluth helped to keep Anna creative, whether his support was psychological or pharmaceutical. In this respect he seems to have served his extraordinarily complex and brilliantly imaginative friend and patient well.

12

Heroin

*

LTHOUGH ANNA KAVAN left no personal record of the beginnings of her heroin addiction, she would appear to have become habituated in the late 1920s, having first experimented with cocaine given to her by a tennis coach in France as a means of heightening her response to the game. Anna graduated on to heroin with its speed-track neural rush of dopamine and sedating effects on the central nervous system as the drug best designed to suppress symptoms of suicidal depression. Tolerance quickly kills off the injected rush and most of the time Anna, like all long-term addicts, would have shot up just to feel normal.

With its terminal connotations – the addict is constantly in danger of overdosing – heroin binds the user to an unconscious suicide pact with the needle or, in Anna's term, her 'bazooka'. The attraction Anna felt to racing car drivers when she was living in the South of France in the 1920s, and in whose company she may well have been introduced to the drug, was the kamikaze dare they entertained in their almost psychopathic desensitization to danger, the sort of life-threatening risk she herself observed each time she depressed the plunger of a loaded hypodermic. Heroin occupies a toxicological category all its own in its irreducible status as a dangerous drug. It is generally considered the bottom – the most degrading of habits for the relentless cycle of need it brokers in the addict. 'Heroin, be the death of me,' Lou Reed intones on the classic Velvet Underground drug song 'Heroin', recorded in Anna's lifetime, playing off his nascent death wish against a rush that has him 'feel just like Jesus' son'.

Heroin is derived from the sap of the opium poppy, *Papaver somniferum*, the pharmaceutical product of synthesized diacetylmorphine. It owes its origins in this form to 1847, when a research chemist called C.R. Alder Wright, working at St Mary's Hospital, Paddington, created the substance by boiling morphine down with an acidic agent. Although additional experiments on diacetylmorphine were done in London and Manchester, it was not until 1898 that the German pharmaceutical company Bayer found a way of making the substance more fat-soluble.

Originally heroin was used as an analgesic to cure morphine addiction, the most common of the opiate dependencies at the time, morphine having become a refined substitute for the nineteenth century's dependency on laudanum, a tincture also prepared from opium. It was the liberal availability of laudanum over the counter and its ubiquitous use that in part fuelled the romantic vision, with Baudelaire, Poe, Coleridge, De Quincey and Keats all becoming habituated to various degrees.

It took less than twenty years for heroin to become a street drug and to filter through to the underground market. Initially it was dispensed legally to intravenous users under a policy of maintenance, by which registered addicts were prescribed heroin by their GPs in the attempt to shield them from the street trade in impure or cut drugs, with the concomitant danger of dirty needles. It was this system that allowed Dr Bluth to prescribe heroin for Anna throughout the years that she remained his private patient.

Where exactly Anna got her drugs in the early years of her dependency is not clear, except that like most addicts she developed an instinctual facility for finding them on the black market. After her fortuitous meeting with Dr Bluth in 1943, the regularity of her supply of clean drugs was assured, and it would seem that Bluth's tendency to over-prescribe allowed her to stockpile the drug.

In the 1950s the existing pattern of maintenance that sustained Anna and most long-term users was starting to change. Throughout the 1950s the official addiction figures in Britain showed not only a steady increase in young heroin users but also an increase in media interest in the subject, so that an issue that had previously attracted little attention as a subculture became a major concern almost overnight. A disturbing new youth culture was emerging. James Dean became a cult hero for his part in the film *Rebel Without a Cause*, as did Marlon Brando for his starring role in *The Wild One*. And Bill Haley's song 'Rock Around the Clock', featured in the 1955 film *Blackboard Jungle*, precipitated the first rock'n'roll-inspired teenage riot in London. When the film was premièred at the Trocadero in London's Elephant and Castle, 'Teddy Boys' went wild and gutted the cinema's interior. Drugs were quickly becoming associated in the public mind with social unrest. In 1958 a gang of nine white youths went on a 'nigger-hunting expedition' in the largely black residential area of Notting Hill. Fired up on a combination of alcohol and amphetamines and armed with knives and wooden staves, they left a trail of badly beaten and injured casualties. The ferocity of these unprovoked attacks was immediately copied by gangs of Teddy Boys, who made organized forays into the black community with a malicious dedication to racially inspired violence.

Although these outbreaks of drug-fuelled atrocity had little to do with Anna's privileged, middle-class life in nearby Kensington, they were indicative of a social problem that because of its link to illicit drug-taking would in time threaten the stability of her source. In May 1951 a young drug user broke into a hospital dispensary just outside London and stole large quantities of morphine, cocaine and heroin. Much of the morphine was recovered, suggesting that the opiate of choice had become heroin. Interestingly, by the end of the decade over sixty heroin users in the London area who traced their habit back to this one episode had been identified. The shadowy figure of the dealer had arrived on London's streets, and smack was starting to gain credibility among a newly intransigent youth set on iconizing the figure of the outlaw as their cult hero.

Most of the younger addicts were gravitating to the West End, where a small number of GPs were becoming known as junkie doctors because of their willingness to prescribe. The most notorious of these was Lady I.M. Frankau, a Wimpole Street psychiatrist, who claimed to have treated approximately five hundred addicts between 1958 and 1964, at a time when the privately habituated Anna was dangerously increasing the intake of the drug, injecting herself every three hours. Personally responsible for prescribing nearly 20 per cent of the heroin in circulation in the country, Lady Frankau inadvertently became one of its major sources of illegal supply as her prescriptions, once dispensed, were often sold on to the street by users who would return for repeat consignments. Given that the Home Office notifications for addicts in 1964, for the UK as a whole, were 753, this is an extraordinary admission, suggesting that Lady Frankau prescribed for the majority of Britain's junkies. It was clear to the public that drugs were no longer a habit subscribed to by decadent aristocrats, bohemians or the dilettante rich, but had become the street currency of a nonconformist youth in search of chemical highs to stimulate their relationship with the R&B music currently popular in the Soho clubs. What Lady Frankau succeeded in doing in her willingness to supply the habituated was to trigger an inevitable reaction from the medical authorities anxious to suppress the official supply in the face of growing media hostility.

Despite the raised social profile of drugs, the report of the first government committee to consider dependency was a model of complacency – superficial in its consideration of the evidence and altogether lacking in vision. The emergence of new drugs such as methadone (physeptone) and the discovery that benzodiazapines (at that time thought to be non-addictive) could be used in the management of heroin withdrawal prompted the government to establish the Interdepartmental Committee on Drug Addiction in 1958, which in turn led to the publication of the first Brain Report in 1961. The report largely glossed the issue of street drugs and attributed the small upward spiral of addicts to increased vigilance on the part of the authorities.

By the time of Dr Bluth's death in 1964 the scene had changed radically. Heroin was widely available in the Soho clubs, and addicts would redeem their scripts at the twenty-four-hour Boots chemists in Piccadilly, waiting until just after midnight in the cafés on Glasshouse Street to have their supplies dispensed for the new day. Although purple hearts (drinamyl or 'speed') remained the select Mod drug, largely because it allowed them to stay up all night at the weekends, heroin quickly established itself as an alternative cool. Smoking it, or 'chasing the dragon', was the usual initiation to heroin, although DCs, dirty cigarettes, never give the user the zippy hit that comes from injecting.

The second Brain Report, published in 1965, had serious consequences for users such as Anna because it finally addressed the issue of the over-prescribing of heroin and cocaine by a small group of London doctors. In future the prescribing of these drugs would require a special licence issued by the Home Office. Licences would normally only be granted to psychiatrists working in specialist treatment units called Drug Dependency Units (DDUs). Anna's DDU was to be the clinic at Charing Cross Hospital under the directorship of Gisella Brigitte Oppenheim, to which she was assigned in the last years of her life.

A clipping found among Anna's papers, relating to the drug clinic to which she was assigned, provides an insight into Gisella Oppenheim's intended non-psychiatric and supportive approach to addicts at the clinic and the methods and environment that Anna found so unnecessarily intrusive into her time and privacy.

The addiction clinic of Charing Cross Hospital, in Central London, lives in a shop across the street from the back entrance of the hospital proper. A plastic sign by the door identifies it as the hospital's 'psychiatric unit annexe'. Within the clinic is a puzzle box of partitions and tiny offices. Gisella Brigitte Oppenheim, director of the clinic since it opened in February 1968, is a briskly sensible psychiatrist, somewhat of the pull-yourself-together-man persuasion. On the spectrum of English clinical opinion, Dr Oppenheim is known to be generally opposed to prescribing heroin.

'I haven't prescribed heroin for a new patient in three years,' she said. 'Most who come into the clinic are poly-drug abusers, and settle for methadone. On heroin, it's much more difficult for them to function in the community. Currently we have only two patients left who are on heroin only. And they are chaotic: it's a full-time job for an addict to be on heroin; injections are necessary every four to six hours, and in their condition, they can take anywhere from twenty minutes to an hour just to get a fix organised . . .

'Our psychiatric approach is supportive and not analytical – perhaps, in American terms, non-psychiatric. We have two full-time social workers. The addicts get a great deal of help with simple practical matters – accommodation, food. The important thing is to teach them that there is an alternative to the way they were living when they first came in. We want them to mix with non-addicts. It is very important to have their leisure time organised. We often find that the addict makes a complete break with the drug-taking group that he has been involved with before he is able to kick the drug habit.'

Almost none of these considerations applied to Anna as a solitary user who had nothing to do with the Piccadilly subculture of street drugs and underworld dealers. Rather than being rehabilitated in the community, her life as a writer demanded she lived outside society.

She kept her fiction relatively free of drug references. Heroin is never directly her subject, and it is largely only in the stories collected in *Julia and the Bazooka*, written in the last years of her life, that she wrote openly of her dependency; when she did, her comments were always positive, as though injecting the drug was usually a cathartic rather than negative experience. Given the time necessary to prepare injections, or what Anna called 'the paraphernalia', as part of the user's metabolic cycle of need, in her later years she must have mostly divided her time between writing and drugs. Rose Knox-Peebles, who on one occasion saw Anna take heroin by lifting the hem of her skirt and injecting herself in the thigh, insists that she accommodated the drug as a normalizing experience, whereas Raymond Marriott witnessed behaviour as bizarre as Anna

throwing a roast chicken across the dinner table before withdrawing to the bedroom where she was discovered picking at a box of chocolates.

Anna's relationship with Bluth was undoubtedly enhanced by his endorse-
ment of her addiction, and it would appear that Anna derived acute gratification
from having Bluth inject her with her 'bazooka', clearly as a means of sublimation.
In the story 'The Zebra-struck' she described her first visit to Bluth's house in
Campden Street after being discharged from hospital.

> She was still not quite stabilized, the margins of reality were not yet distinctly
> marked, she was afraid she might have imagined his sympathetic attitude and
> would now confront someone quite different – someone wearing the usual
> mask-face of non-interest and uncomprehending indifference, which meant
> that no communication was possible. She entered the house, and was taken
> without delay straight to an upper room, where he immediately came forward,
> smiling and giving her both his hands. In a flash all her apprehensions had
> vanished, she knew instantly that everything was all right, he was real, not an
> image she had invented to suit her needs. The relief was so tremendous that she
> was out of herself for a second, floating in sheer happiness, and was surprised
> the next moment to find she'd sat down in a chair.

Her devotion to Bluth never lost the intense thermal of emotional stimulus
that fired their original meeting. Bluth was not only a psychiatrist, well qualified
to cope with emergencies like Anna's erratic tendency to overdose or misregulate
the drug, but he was also effectively Anna's professional dealer. As we have seen,
Bluth was not alone in prescribing heroin for his patients. In 1962 one London
doctor alone prescribed almost 600,000 tablets (6 kg) of heroin for addicts. The
same doctor on one occasion prescribed 900 tablets (9,000 mg) of heroin to one
addict and three days later another 600 'to replace pills lost in an accident'.
According to Rhys Davies, Anna regularly redeemed her prescriptions at Lock-
harts, always making a point of purchasing beauty products at the same time in
the attempt to appear a normal customer.

Among the junkie doctors in London at the time was a dermatologist with a
compulsion to gamble, who ended his medical career issuing prescriptions from
a taxi parked in front of Baker Street tube station. He was arrested for failing to
keep proper records, was given a short prison sentence and finally had his licence
to practise revoked by the General Medical Council. The going price for junkie

doctor prescriptions was between £1 and £2, but their unauthorized circulation helped significantly to create the chaotic drug scene that the government clinic programme was expected to remedy. One psychiatrist, reviewing the years immediately preceding the opening of the clinics, considered that GPs were over-prescribing to such an extent that, for every two addicts receiving prescriptions, at least one other was maintaining his habit from these supplies. It would seem that about a third of the reported addicts were not bona fide addicts but recreational users who persuaded doctors to issue regular prescriptions that they would sell. Contemporary reportage focused on the underworld users at Piccadilly Circus and sensationally to their shooting up in doorways, telephone booths and the toilets in the Underground.

How Anna managed to stockpile huge quantities of heroin in the 1960s is not known, but it would seem to suggest that she had sources other than Bluth. It is common for addicts to register with a number of doctors in order to augment their supply, and in Anna's case the excess was a reassurance that she would not run out, rather than a desire to sell on.

Rhys Davies was invariably circumspect whenever he wrote of Anna's addiction. He alluded to the fact that it was the discipline necessary for sustained writing, as well as a respect for the principles of creative work, that kept her functional and relatively free of the addict's tendency to lie. He recalled an example of Anna's acute paranoia, shown in the extraordinary dislike she took to a waiter at the Café Royal, associating his repellent looks with a hallucinatory figure waiting for her in the foyer. Like many of Anna's other friends, Davies witnessed the unpredictable way she would break off from company to go and fix. 'I had not understood that her brief flight from the restaurant table was done to give herself a shot of heroin, after which she gained detachment from the oppressive hovering of the waiter.' And if her seemingly unshakeable façade of self-control suggested that she suffered no ill consequences from her addiction, then Davies tells us otherwise. 'In moments of acute depression she admitted to grief that she had ever taken to drugs; invulnerability was a mirage.'

Without Bluth, in her last years she was unplugged from her drug mains. She ran the risk of being considered socially dysfunctional and judged for her habit, and according to the new laws she might be subjected to compulsory detoxification. She would not consider methadone as a substitute and continued to attend the clinic at Charing Cross Hospital, at the same time pursuing an abortive search for a private doctor who would be sympathetic to her case.

In pain from a congenital spinal disease and suffering intermittently from the addict's occupational hazard of abscesses as a result of careless injections, she none the less worked efficiently throughout these years. Her application and the brilliantly crafted structure of her work – she was incapable of writing a bad sentence – were the antithesis of the smacked-out, shambolic, rock'n'roll image of heroin cultivated at the time. Nobody pays for a writer's lost time, mistakes or indispositions. The commitment to writing a book must be irrevocable. Anna was true to herself in this respect. She created neither mess, nor half-completions. Her books, and there are twenty of them, are perfectly realized literary constructs that cost time, hard work, rigorous discipline and the extraordinary organization of her singular talent to shape. This small, fragile, deeply traumatized woman wrote without advances and answering only to herself. If heroin altered her brain chemistry, it was not in any way inhibitive or counterproductive to her creativity. It was simply a pharmaceutical coefficient to her energized work quotient. Nothing stopped her from writing, not even during the comparatively dead years of the 1950s and early 1960s when publishers were hard to find and she was largely forgotten. The drug seems to have helped her to manage the sort of deep-seated anxiety that activates hallucination. It was not responsible for the visionary properties of her writings; rather, it helped filter psychic activity that might otherwise have become pathological. Bluth rightly saw no need to confront her dependency, already established for twenty years when they first met in 1943; his judgement seems to have been absolutely justified, given his patient's extraordinary ability to monitor her inner world and channel it into the highly charged visual imagery of her fiction.

In the last decade of Anna's life heroin entered the mainstream of British youth culture via its association with rock music. It had been given its auditory equivalent, along with the image of rock stars like Keith Richards and Eric Clapton going into states of intravenous cryogenics on stage. On a much smaller scale readers of literature would discover drugs and their attendant altered states through the writings of William Burroughs, Allen Ginsberg, Alexander Trocchi, Paul Bowles, Aldous Huxley, Hermann Hesse and, not least, Anna Kavan.

13

In a White Room

*

FTER ANNA KAVAN'S return from South Africa in 1949 her reputation as a writer of imaginative fiction with an aberrant theme fell into temporary abeyance. The largely one-dimensional social realism that pervaded British literature in the 1950s, through the generation of Philip Larkin, Kingsley Amis, John Osborne and John Wain, had little or nothing in common with the European influences at work in Anna's last published novel, the richly poetic and hallucinatory *Sleep Has His House*, in which surrealism and the submerged fact of her addiction had depicted the total isolation of the individual in a world recuperating from death camps, Hiroshima and Nazi atrocities.

Anna had lost direction as a writer and was short of money. The strain was reflected in her turbulent relations with three of her most trusted friends, Dr Bluth, George Bullock and Raymond Marriott. Writing to Marriott, she importuned, 'Please do not try to be antagonized by me. If I seem intolerant or fed up you might remember that probably I'm feeling intolerant of myself.' And she rounded on Bullock in a letter sent on 9 July 1949, 'What on earth has come over you these last few days? Have you and Raymond lost all sense of proportion? As we've known one another such a long time, it's grotesque to envisage me suddenly as some sort of satanic female plotting your ruin.'

Bluth, too, was nurturing grievances over the accumulation of unpaid bills, and while the matter was resolved without any residue of bad feeling, he found it necessary to speak of his frustration in a letter written on 11 June 1949.

> I should give you some idea of what is the matter with me. Theo has her own grievances; and my friends and main patients, whom I was able to help, hold again other strong opinions on you and your family's behaviour, especially after

> I have been crippled by illness . . . Apart from your stepfather's interview and politeness, I never had any answer from your family, with whom to reconcile you I have taken great trouble . . . I beg you to settle what has been left unsettled. You must have some medical and psychological advice; but you must know that I have to disappear completely: otherwise you would antagonize Dr Backus (or whoever he be) on my account.

Bluth was ill at the time with the recurrence of a serious heart condition, and he wanted to be relieved of the onerous task of regularly visiting Anna at home in response to breakdown symptoms and crises relating to her dependency.

Their friendship soon resumed its normal tenor, but the misunderstandings were not so easily patched up with Raymond Marriott and George Bullock. Part of the friction seems to have stemmed from Anna's idea, communicated through Bluth, that Bullock's poor physical and mental health might benefit from the use of heroin or boosts from one of Bluth's individually tailored cocktails of ox blood and methadone. She fought to defend her privileged status as an icon to her gay aficionados.

> Honestly, I've no idea why no one remains my friend. I had (and still have) nothing but warmth and goodwill for you and Raymond, just as for Bluth. I've always tried to help you if there was a chance, and all three of you have told me at various times that I was helpful and that you were attached to me. Yet within the last few weeks all three of you have decided to cut me out of your lives completely; without any adequate explanation; without even taking the trouble to tell me personally what was the matter.

Her persistent financial worries centred on her diminishing income, fixed at £500 per year by her mother, together with a small allowance from her stepfather. She found a minor remedy in forming a small company, Kavan Properties, in the early 1950s, taking an architect called Andrew Salmon as her partner. The business proved successful within limits, the object being to buy, refurbish according to Anna's distinct all-white aesthetic and renovate houses, mostly in the Peel Street and Campden Street area of Kensington in which Anna lived.

Undeterred by the poor critical reception given *Sleep Has His House*, Anna continued to write for three hours each morning before devoting the remainder of the day to her business enterprises. Her dedication as a writer and her insistence on going through multiple drafts were recorded by Raymond Marriott, who described in detail her assiduous working method:

Anything she wrote could take several months to several years to finish. She drafted everything at least six times. First, after taking notes, she would write out a draft by hand and then recopy this into a second MS after extensive revision. Then, she would either recopy the piece by hand, or if it had reached the right stage, she would have it typed into a MS, with a carbon, both of which she would edit extensively. Then another typed copy would be made and this one checked and redefined. More revisions could be made or a final draft could be typed.

In 1954 Anna broke a six-year silence and submitted a story, 'Happy Name', to *Encounter* magazine, whose editor John Lehmann is reputed to have accepted it for publication with the comment, '*The* Anna Kavan? Why, I thought she was dead.' In the story a panicky, ageing spinster regresses in a dream to a childhood spent in a rambling Victorian house, giving Anna the opportunity to explore the sort of interior geography common to all serious opiate users such as Poe, De Quincey and Coleridge, in which a complex of passages telescopes in on some unnameable catastrophe at its centre.

A sequence of quickly dissolving views passed before her mind's eye; the wings and turrets, all the odd bays and excrescences, added at different epochs, with their labyrinthine connecting passages, their anterooms, steps up or down; all the complicated geography of the outlying parts of the mansion, in use, or crumbling into decay. It wasn't easy to find the way through . . .

However, this brief, unnoticed return to print did nothing to reverse the impression that as a writer Anna Kavan belonged to a largely forgotten past.

Without hope of publication she continued to work on her next novel, *A Scarcity of Love*. In 1955 she received the news that her mother had died at the Tevis mansion in Monterey. Her pathologically jealous mother, who would credit her daughter with no personal achievements – it is unlikely she ever read Anna's books – was in part Anna's invincible adversary, and in part the provider of her only regular income. Expecting to benefit financially from her mother's will, Anna was understandably shocked to find herself effectively disinherited. She contested the will, in which her mother had left all her money to her husband, leaving Anna only a share of the proceeds from the sale of the house at Earley. The blow was additionally catastrophic in that she lost any statutory right to her allowance. In fact this continued to be paid right to the end of her life, owing to her stepfather's generosity in recognizing Anna's needs as a marginalized writer forced to the edge financially by her overriding commitment to her art.

Anna inherited a few insignificant effects from her mother's house, including a number of miniatures and her mother's gilded harp, which she displayed as a decorative feature of her living-room first at 99 Peel Street and later at 19 Hillsleigh Road. Perversely, she also retained a portrait of her mother by the kitsch painter, Vladimir Tretchikoff, showing the 65-year-old woman fully made up and frozen into an immutably youthful middle age, sitting at an easel, paintbrush in hand; perhaps this was a masochistic reminder of the superficial, self-regarding and eminently self-satisfied woman who had also been a mother consistently disparaging of her daughter's failures and indifferent to her success.

In the novel *A Scarcity of Love*, which Anna published in the same year as her mother died, she rewrites the story of her disinheritance. Her mother is cast as the parasitical Regina, married to a much younger man.

> The rich woman had willed the house with all its contents, the whole estate, almost her entire fortune to the chauffeur. To her husband she left only a meagre life interest, a pittance; and some objects without any special value, as keepsakes.

Anna put up £50 to have the novel published by Angus Downie, who as previously noted went bankrupt almost simultaneously with the book's appearance. Springing to her assistance, as the book had been well received by reviewers, Raymond Marriott published a notice in *The Stage*.

> Authoress in a most unusual plight is Miss Anna Kavan. Her novel *A Scarcity of Love* was given high praise by reviewers; a big public demand followed. But only 500 copies are available for distribution. Mr Oliver Moxon, a fellow author, and managing director of a book distributing firm, tells me the situation has arisen because of the difficulties encountered by the publisher after review copies had been sent out. 'My heart bleeds for Miss Kavan,' he said. 'It is her first book for eight years, and, like her last, *Sleep Has His House*, deals with the tragedy of a woman of abnormal mentality.' Now Mr Moxon is trying to arrange a second printing.

A Scarcity of Love is Anna's allegorical reworking, almost in the form of a surreal fairy tale, of the story of a daughter, Gerda, who suffers implacable belittlement at the hands of her malevolent and reproachful mother. The repressive Regina lacks the emotional capacity for nurture, and she projects a negative capability that results in Gerda's chronic lack of self-esteem and mistrust of life.

Distrusting the ephemeral and precarious nature of happiness, she was afraid to make any claim on even a happy memory: preferring to retire into her private fantasy world; trying neither to think of her real situation, nor to make contact with human beings.

The novel's intensely subjective vision, approximating to what Rhys Davies called a personal mythology rather than an assemblage of facts drawn from the real world, was in many ways a continuity, although a modified one, of the dream dissolves Anna had employed in *Sleep Has His House*.

With the same compulsive gravitation towards death that seems to have gripped Anna herself for most of her life, Gerda drowns herself rather than continue with her sense of extreme alienation.

With sudden intensity, she longed to escape from all the sadness, the guilt and the not-being-loved, of the world to which she had come unwanted, where nobody wished her to stay . . . She had a vague notion that she was to blame for her own unhappiness. But she no longer understood how this was so. She could no longer remember what she had done wrong – the things left undone, unsaid . . . It all seemed far away . . . long ago . . . not so very important. She knew she had always been stupid: there had always been so much she did not understand . . . and no one had ever explained. But now it seemed not to matter much any more.

Most copies of *A Scarcity of Love* were pulped, and the book was not reprinted until three years after Anna's death, in 1971, when Rhys Davies, praising its imaginative firepower, drew parallels between its predominantly imaginative landscapes and the altered topology of *Ice*:

In *A Scarcity of Love*, as in her novel *Ice*, she discards such aids to realism as geographical facts or mundane physical details; even time seems to have halted in a menacing country of the emotions where the very ground is uneasy with seismic-like threats. There is a truthful exactitude in Anna Kavan's mapping of this personal milieu. Anna Kavan's talent for extracting an austere beauty from intimations of doom is as compelling here as in so much of her greatly admired work.

To add to the disappointment surrounding the publication of *A Scarcity of Love*, Anna found her nerves stretched to breaking point by the turbulent process of moving house from 47 Campden Street – the street in which Dr Bluth also lived – round the corner to 99 Peel Street in Kensington. The house needed rewiring, and Anna wrote to George Bullock of the temporary but troubling inconvenience. 'To say I hope you're better seems absurd, so I can only hope you're at least not any worse. Had you come over today you wouldn't have been able to work, as in addition to Alan and his 3 men and another independent electrician, Salmon had sent that Negro from Watts.' There were also the unwelcome practical details of business demanding her attention, and Anna's dislike of protocol had her write to Raymond Marriott, 'I'm sorry not to have arranged anything with you before, but, as you may have heard from George, there has been rather a turmoil lately with income tax people and other horrors . . .' Anna bought most of her books locally at the Bodkin Bookshop in Notting Hill Gate, a shop run by Diana Johns, who was sympathetic to the sort of fiction published by the newly emerging independents such as Peter Owen and John Calder, proponents of experimental fiction. It was Diana Johns who originally put Peter Owen in touch with Anna Kavan in 1956, mentioning her as a customer who was also a prestigious author who had made her reputation in the 1940s and was now in search of a publisher for her latest novel, *Eagles' Nest*. Diana Johns facilitated a meeting between Anna and Peter Owen, who accepted the manuscript and quickly moved to bring the book out in 1957.

Susan Payne, who worked at the Bodkin Bookshop at the time, remembers Anna as a regular customer, somewhat inscrutable, always elegantly dressed in pastel-coloured suits to match her platinum hair and pale pink lipsticks and exchanging few words with anyone but the proprietor. The bookshop was also a lending library to which Anna belonged. Susan's husband John Payne recollects Anna's absolutely translucent skin, as though each vein was visible beneath the surface, as well as her imperious manner at parties. Anna was usually accompanied on such occasions by her solicitous secretary, George Bullock, who looked after her personal needs. To John Payne she had the junkie's cold aura, the remoteness of the hardened user dependent, above all else, on her next shot; while Rhys Davies's brother Lewis recalls her as already ruined by drugs, conspicuously overdressed in a fur coat, visiting Peter Maranca's patisserie in New Compton Street to buy what were considered to be the best millefeuilles in London, sticky pink and white wedge-shaped artefacts tiered with a high-rise filling of jam and cream.

Something of the tortuous complexity of Anna's often overstrained relations with her principal gay friends, Rhys Davies, Raymond Marriott and George Bullock, can be assessed in her regular correspondence with the three, in which reproaches for negligence on their part alternate with contrition on hers for misbehaving at times – most often owing to drugs. The continuous oscillations in her friendship with Rhys Davies, fluctuations that always returned to a secure axis of friendship, are nowhere better highlighted than in the itemized letter Anna sent him from Peel Street on 24 March 1957. Her fractious sensitivity to rejection is carried to extremes. Distressed by Davies's most recent letter, she begins by stating that she has let time elapse before replying, so as to be objective in her response.

My comments on your main points are:

You proposed bringing the V. Bakers to see me. I'm not aware of having expressed any desire for this meeting, though I do remember saying that, if it had to take place, I would prefer to be spared the complications of vegetarian food.

Is one not allowed to voice a complaint about anything, even to a friend of 20 yrs standing? After all, you make pretty definite demands on your friends, don't you?

I presume this is a joke about St Cecilia's day?

My 'menacing greeting' was a genuine act of friendliness; knowing how you dislike being involved with other people's emotions, I gave you the chance of escaping mine, if you wished.

I quite agree, social life does require concessions to others and disciplinary action against the ego. Surely, the whole point of friendship is that one waives the requirements of the world in general?

The main thing seems to be that you set a higher value on a kind of impersonal gregariousness than on friendship – in this I could never agree with you.

It would have been quite possible for me to welcome you as an old friend then, or at any other time; but apparently your relations with the V. Bakers are more important, and for me to receive them then would have involved an effort I consider intolerable and unrewarding.

What you call discipline in general social relations is all right, but unbearable if allowed to de-personalize friendship and deprive it of its significance.

Although Anna stops short of risking the friendship through outright recrimination, her tendency to analyse ruthlessly suggests the seriousness she attached to her closed and viciously competitive circle of friends and how the value she places on integrity, rather than superficiality, is at the heart of the matter. There is just the right edge of constrained bitchiness apparent in the mix, too, suggesting that she could give good repartee in return for the camp ripostes that were the natural expression of her friends.

Eagles' Nest, published in 1957, sounded an altogether new note in British fiction, in that the direct influence of Kafka on Anna's writing is also inflected with traces of the *nouveau roman* that she had assimilated through her reading of the novels of Alain Robbe-Grillet, Claude Simon and Marguerite Duras, proponents of a distinctly European genre of fiction. True to Kafka, the novel's ambiguous protagonist finds himself at the nadir of his career, working as an advertising artist in a department store, blaming bad luck and global unrest for his depressed situation. Capitalizing on her theme of the disaffected individual exposed to altered geography in a world where state boundaries have dissolved into ubiquitous totalitarianism, Anna has her narrator explain:

I had always done so well in my chosen profession, nothing could have seemed more promising than my future, or more secure when I was abruptly discharged, through no fault of mine, but because a reduction in personnel became necessary, and chance was allowed to decide who should go. How could I help feeling aggrieved and embittered by such disastrous bad luck?

In order to escape the degrading demands made on him by routine employment, the narrator accepts the offer of a job as library assistant to 'the Administrator' of a large estate called Eagles' Nest in a nameless tropical country. On arrival the protagonist finds that the Administrator is absent, and in a manner reminiscent of Kafka's *The Castle*, he is subjected to quangos of functionaries and the meaningless quotient of bureaucracy. The hero's sustained belief that in spite of the invidious system at work at Eagles' Nest he will encounter revelatory mystical experiences gives rise to some of Anna's great visionary passages in which entire landscapes are hallucinated into existence. The white-hot tempo of the writing, together with the unnerving beauty at its core, results in scenes of often blindingly translucent vision, placing her alongside J.G. Ballard as the British contemporary novelist with whom she shared disruptive, shape-shifting affinities.

> But it was from somewhere in the far reaches of imagination that I watched the whiteness above the summits meet and extend, forming a straight line that ran the whole length of the range. This white line remained fixed; while from it a cloudy deluge began to pour down, a weird white soundless Niagara streaming out of the sky. Materializing from nowhere, out of the otherwise cloudless blue, the incredible torrent instantly obliterated the mountains and came sweeping on, overwhelming everything as it came. Though I was directly in its path, what I felt was awe, not alarm, as though the astounding cataract did not threaten me personally: and, sure enough, it halted a few yards from my window. There, for no reason that I could see, the cloud began coiling back on itself, slowly evaporating in upward spray.

The entire imaginative landscape of *Eagles' Nest*, with its mountains 'all of the same stark, forbidding outline, flat-topped, rectilinear, savagely coloured and depthless-looking, as if painted on the cobalt sky; crowding one behind another like a gigantic city of vast skyscrapers, or a monstrous cemetery of colossal coffins stood up on end' is an inimitable triumph of poetic vision on Anna's part, a world so individual as to place her at the cutting edge of 1950s' British fiction, as remote from her mainstream contemporaries as the idea of a UFO doing a flyover above Notting Hill.

The *New Yorker* has called her 'a writer of such chillingly matter-of-fact, unself-pitying vigour that her vision transcends itself'. In many ways *Eagles' Nest* is Anna's most successful attempt to fuse inner and outer realities into a seamlessly interchangeable whole. The solitary vision she had lived with for decades as an artist too individual to be absorbed into her times now found its composite expression. The narrator's anticipation of stepping through a gateway, and having his inner state succeed in projecting a psychic condition into reality, was very much Anna's hope as a visionary writer.

Now I remembered having already received intimations of this second secret existence, though only in the form of vague hints I had chosen to disregard. Today for the first time the other aspect of things had revealed itself fully, with a reality far beyond that of dreaming, so that I seemed to be living two lives at once. I noticed, though, that I never seemed fully aware of them both together; for now the concrete world regained the ascendancy, excluding the dream world beyond, but not obliterating my memory of it completely.

Sales of *Eagles' Nest* were small. The novel appeared infelicitously at the height of the Movement's popularity – this was the age of the 'Angry Young Men' and of the emergence of a literature that made the grey plateau of pedestrianism its cause and elevated the lower-middle-class, university-educated misfit into its hero. The sociological discontent of the new literary generation, the cerebral being given dominance over the imaginative and the boundaries of formal limitations given precedence over imaginatively conceived experience, meant nothing to Anna.

Eagles' Nest was followed a year later by the publication of a book of short stories, *A Bright Green Field*. Owing largely to editorial misinterpretations about the direction of her fiction, and a certain suspicion on Peter Owen's part that her increasing subjectivity was taking her too far inwards as a novelist, it was another eight years before he accepted a new book from her.

The problem of solitary experience – Anna neither had nor wanted contemporaries as a writer – and how it filters through to an author's subject matter, sometimes amplifying imagination in direct relation to a loss of hold on reality, was explored by one of Anna's most enthusiastic readers, Anaïs Nin, in a diary entry early in 1959. Nin wrote: 'Anna Kavan, with all her brilliance, has gone too far into the exploration of the labyrinths without renewing her oxygen supply through life. She seems to have stopped living, and is moving into an impasse. I admire her and only fear sterility for her later.' She was to be proved wrong by the regenerative faculties shown by Anna in her last two published books, *Who Are You?* (1963) and *Ice* (1967), but Anna herself was undeniably aware that heroin and a generic need for a solitary life were working both for and against her. Writing to Rhys Davies from Peel Street, she was forced to defend her inveterate antisocial tendencies by stating the facts of her life.

It must be tiresome, of course, if another person doesn't fit in with your timetable of starting the evening at 9 o'clock. But it is possible, you know, that one might feel ill and depressed and so have difficulties fitting in. I should have thought you would see, with your writer's insight, that, for an introverted unsociable solitary person like myself, who has been alone all day in an unreal world of whatever I'm writing, to suddenly snap out of it at that time of the evening and try to be sociable, requires a colossal effort.

As the 1950s came to an end she had succeeded in pulling herself back from relative literary extinction, reasserting her reputation in small ways, suggesting that she was still there, resistant and capable of renewal.

14

Love Minus Zero:
Kavan and the 1960s' Zeitgeist

*

IN THE EARLY 1960s, as though antici-
pating the apocalyptic zeitgeist of a decade characterized by violently disruptive
social changes, Anna Kavan began work on a novel she provisionally called 'The
Cold World'. The book's title, symptomatic of her addiction and the increasing
sense of isolation she felt as a person and writer, was to undergo mutation to 'The
Ice World', before finally becoming *Ice*, one of the many concessions she made in
the course of the book's radical editorial makeover.

Ice is of course Anna's heroin novel, in the same way as the Rolling Stones'
Exile on Main Street is permeated by Keith Richards's opiated power chords as
its drug signature. Boundaries between hallucination and reality are constantly
dissolved in *Ice*, so that the narrative appears discontinuous, its linear structure
constantly undermined by flashbacks and the interiorization of events at the
expense of a developing storyline.

The 1960s found Anna living at 19 Hillsleigh Road, suitably insulated from
reality by the Kensington house she designed and built, and occupying the L-
shaped upstairs flat, 19a, while the lower floor was let initially to Gerald Hamilton
and later to her friend Raymond Marriott. The move from Peel Street to Hillsleigh Road, undertaken at a time of torrential autumn rain, had been hugely
demanding on Anna's energies, and her general lack of practical resources often
left her at the mercy of builders. She wrote to Rhys Davies to tell him something
of the relief she felt as the ordeal neared its end.

At last the chaos of the move is subsiding – it's been quite the most fearful one I've
ever experienced, all sorts of unexpected difficulties and complications to con-
tend with, as well as the perpetual torrents of rain. I feel quite exhausted but rather
strong, as if I've experienced an enormously complex campaign of some kind.

She was also critically short of money and expressed her thanks in a letter to Davies for his generous support.

> Thanks most awfully for the cheque – I think it's very generous of you, though I feel I ought not to take it. However, being in this ghastly financial mess, I do so with great pleasure – every 6d is welcome! I've got to complete on Monday and not a hope of raising the money – God knows what will happen.

From her flat in Hillsleigh Road, with its walled garden and white Venetian blinds shutting out the day, Anna could pick up on the ambient surf of traffic issuing from Holland Park Avenue on the Notting Hill Gate side and Kensington Church Street on the other, while remaining relatively free of noise pollution in her chosen location. *Ice* was written, so to speak, in a W8 interzone, a space in which she could interact with the city while at the same time keeping herself at a remove from its crazy, hyped-up dynamic. With the gold weathercock on the spire of the neighbouring St George's Church, on Campden Hill, elevated above her property, Anna was probably unaware that another platinum-haired diva, equally guarded about her private life, the pop singer Dusty Springfield, was almost her neighbour around the corner at 38 Aubrey Walk.

Anna's need to bury the fact of her addiction and to maximize the time available in which to write – she was now approaching sixty – had her settle for a lifestyle and property in which quiet and privacy were priorities. Like the imposing white façade of the house, the garden also served as an exclusion factor and was densely cultivated as an additional screen between Anna and the world. There were fig trees, decaying elders, rhododendrons that exploded into purple flower, straggly waterfalls of wistaria, faded pink tea roses and an idiosyncratic cocktail of tall grasses, shrubs and laurel bushes. Anna, who did the gardening herself, also cultivated a herb garden and grew spring onions, mint, parsley, bay and sage and would sit outside and write on a grey-painted bench peeling to bare bleached wood. It was from a house with an interior every bit as complex as the sometimes labyrinthine corridors of her fiction that she began work on a series of novels and short stories that would occupy the last decade of her life. Increasingly preoccupied by a life comprising disciplined work and the private rituals built into an orderly domestic routine, she achieved a new liberating incentive in her writing.

No character in *Ice* is given a name. Peter Owen's initial criticism of 'The

Cold World', that 'the characters do not really come to life', is valid only in the sense that they appear bleached of human characteristics. Part of the problem with *Ice* gaining acceptance appears to have been editorial obtuseness. Anna's visionary facility was too far advanced for her editor Philip Inman, who actually visited Anna at Hillsleigh Road on several occasions to work on restructuring the book. Anna's correspondence with Peter Owen about the novel's imaginary landscapes and deliberately interiorized action also manifests extreme frustration at what she felt was Owen's inability to understand her intentions. In the splinter-book *Mercury*, not published until 1994 but originally forming part of the manuscript of 'The Cold World', Anna not only names the three principal characters as Luke, Luz and Chas but maps out their psychological profiles in ways that are humanly rather than post-humanly convincing. As the baseline to *Ice*, *Mercury* coruscates with a richer poetic imagery than its meticulously reworked successor. If the writing in *Ice* has the translucency of vodka, *Mercury* adds tinctures of prismatic colour to the clear spirit.

Whatever Anna's mental state at the time of writing *Ice*, the book's temperature reflects her own incurable subordination to heroin. It is a white-on-white text that portrays a compulsively sadomasochistic relationship in a world escalating into global catastrophe. It seems somehow to have intersected directly with the revolutionary spirit of the 1960s. Anticipating John Lennon's affirmation 'Nothing is real' in the lyrics to the Beatles' 'Strawberry Fields for Ever', the hallucinatory dissolves in *Ice* question the entire nature of reality in the way that a generation adapting to psychedelics looked to inner exploration as an antidote to materialism. Anna, too, was busy sighting the altered dimensions of inner space as a route out of the impending global catastrophe she sensed.

> He told me about the hallucination of space-time, and the joining of past and future so that either could be the present, and all ages accessible. He said he would take me to his world, if I wanted to go. He and others like him had seen the end of our planet, the end of the human race. The race was dying, the collective death-wish, the fatal impulse to self-destruction, though perhaps human life might survive. The life here was over. But life was continuing and expanding in a different place. We could be incorporated in this wider life, if we chose.

During the time that Anna was writing 'The Cold World' London exploded into cool. A new fashion-obsessed Mod youth, dressed by John Stephen's chain of shops in Carnaby Street, blocked on pills, riding flashy mirror-stacked Lambrettas around Soho and wired to the rapidly expanding R&B club circuit, had initiated both a gender war and a generational divide. With the image and music of London bands such as the Rolling Stones, the Pretty Things, the Kinks, the Who and the Small Faces spearheading a hipster revolt triggered by social disdain, the moral restraint that had characterized Anna's generation was blown apart for ever. Amphetamines, or purple hearts, the Mod drug of choice, were soon complemented on the London club scene by psychoactives and hallucinogens – particularly cannabis and LSD – as potential gateways to a substance-induced vision. Youth had gone chemical.

No matter how indi ..dy the revolution filtered through to Anna, in her overheated apa ` ι with its Burmese gong acting as a coffee-table and her mother's gild ρ, she was living in a city that was the epicentre of cataclysmic social unrest. For almost the entire last decade of her life Anna's unconscious found itself interfacing with the city's ruptured psyche, her stream of hallucinated imagery reflected in the mind-set and weird psychogeography of a re-visioned capital.

'The Cold World', and the two visionary novels it generated, are in part a fictionalized account of Anna's travels in Norway, California, New Zealand, Bali, New York and South Africa during the Second World War, a post-survivor travelogue resituated in her novel as a nameless, unidentifiable terrain that is in the process of being transformed into a blinding, nuclear white-out.

What is remarkable about *Ice*, the novel extracted from 'The Cold World' manuscript, is that it has no predecessors in British fiction, and while it owes something of its dystopian vision to Kafka's world of depersonalized administration, presided over by essentially psychopathic despots, it is essentially a one-off, a rogue cell menacing the ordered pattern of British fiction. Anna was normal in her world but abnormal to an establishment that continued to value social realism over and above the transformative powers of imagination. Only J.G. Ballard in his early novels like *The Drowned World*, *The Drought* and *The Crystal World* had explored similarly hallucinated landscapes, in which an internal vision corresponds to the distinct possibilities of an irremediably shattered world.

Early versions of 'The Cold World' met with resistance. Disappointed by Peter Owen's failure to commit to early drafts of the book Anna offered it to Calder and Boyars, who despite expressing an interest none the less rejected the manuscript. In late 1965 another version was submitted to Weidenfeld and Nicolson by Francis King, who was working for them at the time as a literary adviser, only to be turned down, despite his strong recommendation.

With Peter Owen still unwilling to make a definite offer of publication, Anna was forced to defend her position in an eloquent statement of where she stood as a writer.

> I appreciate your only wanting to print my best work, but you always make comparisons with something I did in the past, as if there was an absolute standard of good writing which didn't change. Even if this is so, I can't keep on all my life writing in the same way. Unless I feel a compulsion to write a book in a certain way before I start, I know it won't be any good, so I can only write as I want to. *A Scarcity of Love* was what I wanted to write, and the best writing I could do at that time. The world is now quite different and so is my life in it. One reacts to the environment and atmosphere one lives in, one absorbs outside influences, and my writing changes with the conditions outside. The kind of adventure story seems to be in the air just now, which is probably why I wanted to write a book of that sort in my own language and with my own symbolism. It is not meant to be realistic writing. It's a sort of present day fable, in which detailed characterisation would be out of place.

If one of heroin's functions is to trigger the release of dopamine in the brain's reward centre, then Anna's tolerance to its effects had by the time she came to write *Ice* turned her drug-taking into a process designed to offset withdrawal rather than to kick in heady dopamine rushes. Heroin had bonded with her innate nihilism in confirming the dystopian vision of the cold universe pervading her fiction. But independent of her habit and strictly imposed solitude Anna never lost sight of the importance of beauty in her life. There's an aesthetic to her work, like her carefully designed appearance, that is often hard, brilliant and durable as a diamond.

In a memorable passage in *Ice* she observes, 'It was snowing slightly, and the complex structure of each individual snowflake appeared in crystalline clearness, the delicate starlike, flowerlike forms perfectly distinct and as bright as jewels.' It is the absolute visual clarity of her spellbinding imagery, together with the powerful vision behind it, that makes Anna the equal of women writers like Virginia Woolf, Anaïs Nin, Jean Rhys, Jane Bowles, Sylvia Plath and Jeanette

Winterson, to name some of the outstanding proponents of the poetic novel in women's fiction.

Her work on 'The Cold World' was interrupted catastrophically in March 1964 by the death of her personal mentor and psychiatrist, Dr Bluth. Anna's dependency on Bluth, not only as the source of her privately scripted heroin but as an inseparable friend, who despite his marriage offered her the intellectual stimulus and the emotional support of a partner, was as acute as her habit. Bluth and the drug he supplied to modify Anna's pathological fear of breakdown and deep-seated depression were symbiotically linked in Anna's mind. His sudden death after years of cardiac problems smashed a hole clean through Anna's defences like a boulder shattering thin ice. The strength of their relationship, which was founded on a mutually observed independence reinforced by absolute trust in the durability of their bond, extended to their having agreed on a suicide pact.

Without Bluth, Anna's world froze into the alienated, endgaming states that occupied her writing. Dutiful to the last, she composed herself sufficiently to write a short obituary for *The Times*, honouring her friend.

The death in London last week of Dr Karl Theodor Bluth, the poet, playwright and essayist, should not pass unnoticed. Dr Bluth, whose anti-fascist views forced him to leave Germany in 1934, was principally known in this country as a medical consultant and a psychiatrist, though among his publications are two long essays in the periodical *Horizon*, 'The Revival of Schelling' and 'Swiss Humanism', and a book *Leibnitz the European*, published by Drummond. Many British poets and painters were his patients as well as other refugees, all of whom found in him an unfailing source of stimulation and encouragement.

After drawing up her will, dividing her main estate between Raymond Marriott and Rhys Davies, she attempted to overdose on a massive heroin shot but was discovered by Marriott and rushed to hospital. 'I was desperate, determined not to go on living,' she wrote.

In front of those who were left, I put on an act and concealed my intention. But, accidentally, or thinking one of my so-called friends, really was well-disposed towards me, I must have given some indication of what I meant to do. So these people frustrated me, forced me to live my impossible life and go on suffering. I can't say how profoundly I resent their interference. I write this to prevent any misunderstanding.

Her general health was starting to deteriorate, and she observed her decline with philosophic detachment. That she wanted to die is forcibly expressed in a letter written to Rhys Davies around the time of Bluth's death.

For the last day or two I've been stricken with one of those mysterious infections, which I suppose all come from my skin poisoning me. Or perhaps I've just 'gone on shite', after working so hard and having so many setbacks. Anyway, I still have a fairly high temperature, can't work or do anything else. So forgive me for not ringing up . . . It is humiliating in the extreme at my age, to start watching myself falling to bits. There's no doubt suicide is the only course consonant with human dignity. The devilish thing is that one seems to become cowardly with age – or perhaps even the death wish weakens; like everything else.

But to think of Anna's world as singularly depressive is a misconception. Emotionally damaged by two failed marriages, the survivor of numerous breakdowns and serious suicide attempts, progressively impoverished when she had once been wealthy, dependent on a Class A drug and living very much alone as a woman in her sixties, her courage was none the less compounded by the need to write. She had to keep writing and finish *Ice*, the defiant affirmation of a creative gift that transcended all the aberrant traits of psychopathology. She manifested obdurate courage in devoting herself post-Bluth to completing this task and to working on the stories published posthumously in the collections *Julia and the Bazooka* and *My Soul in China*.

There were moments of pleasure, too, principally taken sitting outside writing in the conspiratorial garden, the city carried to her on the air-waves and pushing like a sonic tide at her walls. One such incident was made into the subject of the short story 'A Town Garden', in which Anna described her immediate territory with a deep sense of physically belonging.

The day is warm, grey and quiet. I sit on the bench from which nearly all the paint has peeled off. My garden is the size of a largish room, and seems enclosed like a room, on account of the walls all round it . . . The wall behind the bench is the wall of my house. On the left is the grey, windowless wall of the house next door, on which an old dying vine has traced the obscure calligraphy of its twisted stems. Ten-foot brick walls, trees and bushes are on the other two sides. Overshadowed like this the garden gets little sun, and today there's no sun at all, and therefore no shadow. Although the earth and the stones are quite dry, my impression is of a dark, damp room, full of deep shade, as it might be full of water.

Anna was one of those solitary practitioners of the novel who, going it alone and working oblivious to literary fashions, often use the experience of breakdowns encountered along the way as the basis for their work. Such writers usually find their strength by turning inwards and making writing itself into the art of survival. Anna lived to write, and the manuscript of 'The Cold World' became the white moon map she obsessively crossed and re-crossed in her solitary Kensington days. Writing ahead of her time, she would never live to see *Ice* or her largely forgotten and long out of print books *Asylum Piece* and *Sleep Has His House* taken up as underground classics by the drug subculture evolving out of the 1960s. Like Proust, Anna used all her significant experience as subject matter for her work, making the little event big and spontaneous perception into thought images. It was this facility that had Raymond Marriott say of her, 'When Anna would look out of a window she could see more in a minute than most would in a lifetime. She was extraordinarily perceptive, intuitive, visionary.'

As she busily stockpiled heroin in her bathroom cabinet at Hillsleigh Road Anna picked up unconsciously on the fact that she now lived in a city in which recreational drugs were a common even if illegal currency, a fact that was drawing unwelcome attention to habituated users like herself. Apprehensive of impending changes in legislation, she expressed her serious concern to Raymond Marriott. 'I've been listening to that bloody Lady Frankau. What a bitch. You know there's a plan now to stop addicts getting supplies from doctors even if they are on the Home Office list – i.e. to introduce compulsory "disintoxication" for everyone.'

In the first half of the 1960s London was predominantly an amphetamine capital. The Mods made speed into a recreational drug, and Parliament responded by passing legislation in 1964 especially for the purpose of classifying it as an illegal substance. We do not know where Kavan obtained it to counteract the depressive effects of heroin, other than through Bluth, but Rhys Davies assures us that the stimulant was part of her personally designed pharmaceutical regime. One of the main sources for the drug on a street level was the Scene Club, situated in Ham Yard in Great Windmill Street, Soho. Drinamyl pills were sold there at the equivalent of 6p each but were usually bought in fives, tens, twenties, fifties and hundreds. Dealers also operated from La Discothèque in Wardour Street, the Mod hotspot the Marquee, the clubs along Greek Street and a stand outside Tiffany's. Most of the pills in circulation came in through the London docks and had the manufacturer's name SKF (Smith, Kline and French) stamped on them as a mark of authenticity.

The world of amphetamine clubs was not Anna's social scene, although she asked to be taken to one in order to experience first hand the drugs on offer and the music driving the newly liberated youth. Many of these clubs constellated around the D'Arblay Street grid of Soho and included a gay venue called Le Douce and others within yards of each other with names like the Subway, the Coffee Pot, the Huntsman, the Limbo Club, the Granada and Take Five. It was in clubs like these that a devotionally Mod youth first experienced the music of the Who. Songs such as 'I Can't Explain', 'My Generation' and 'Anyway, Anywhere, Anyhow' were taken up as the youthfully intransigent expression of a highly fashion-conscious pillhead cult electrified by Pete Townshend's trashing of his guitars on stage and the ritual destruction of the band's equipment by way of apocalyptic finale to an explosive Marquee set.

If Anna's relatively sedate, middle-class Kensington neighbourhood seemed the antithesis of the wired, clubby West End ethos, and her privileged education at Malvern Girls' College an anachronism to the foppish King's Road crowd, her books were her means of imaginatively subverting her past. Her writing about the brutally sadomasochistic sex explored by Luz and her glacially detached partners in 'The Cold World' is always explicit, which was uncommon among women writers of her generation. Anna makes it clear that Luz is compliant with the violence perpetrated on her body and actually finds an emotional reward in being violated, preferring possession of any kind to the agonized state of feeling otherwise totally alienated from life. How much of this is autobiographical, we do not know. As we have noted, her marriage to Donald Ferguson appeared to have been conducted on an unequal sexual basis and possibly involved marital rape. The residual legacy of physical revulsion and emotional damage that Anna carried from the two years she spent with Ferguson seems to have stayed with her for the rest of her life and filtered through to the frigidly compliant but mechanically sadomasochistic sex scenes in 'The Cold World'. Even taking into account that heroin depresses libido, sex in Anna's novels is never consensual but, rather, the expression of extreme violence in which the man's unilateral gratification succeeds only in alerting the passive female to the possibilities of deriving pleasure from perversity. Even if Anna did not actually experience sado-masochistic sex in her life, it was certainly a compulsive fantasy. She told her friend Rose Knox-Peebles that she found men boring, a statement Knox-Peebles took to mean sexually. In 'The Cold World', and in *Ice*, the male is portrayed as the predator and the female as the half-compliant victim.

> Later she did not move, gave no indication of life, lying exposed on the ruined bed as on a slab in a mortuary. Sheets and blankets spilled on the floor, trailed over the edge of the dais. Her head hung over the edge of the bed in a slightly unnatural position, the neck twisted in a way that suggested violence, the bright hair twisted into a sort of rope by his hands. He sat with his hand upon her, asserting his right to his prey. When his fingers passed over her naked body, lingering on thighs and breasts, she was shaken by a long painful shudder; then she went still again.

In 'The Cold World' sex takes place in silence. There are no words prefacing it and no attempt afterwards to explain or in any way justify the brutal nature of the assault. Luz, Anna's fictional persona in both *Ice* and *Mercury*, seems conditioned to violence, as she herself may have been programmed by Ferguson. She is tied up in cord when she models nude for her artist husband Chas, is verbally slapped, has her wrists dislocated and is repeatedly sexually abused. The glacial tone of the sexual encounters in 'The Cold World' has something in common with Pauline Réage's pornographic novel, *The Story of O*, in that both books depict sex as a ruthlessly mechanical pursuit devoid of emotions or sensuality and in which the female learns to transform pain and humiliation into a form of tolerated masochism. By actively submitting to her aggressor Luz undermines the pleasure she derives from force. It is her way of reversing the power roles in a vicious relationship and of limiting her partner's potential for escalating violence.

Somewhere within Anna were the deeply incised emotional scars of a battered woman, who mistrusted heterosexual men and their motives to the point of excluding them wherever possible from her life. That she had been unwillingly a mother too had undoubtedly contributed substantially to her growing aversion to conventional relationships. It is difficult to imagine this impractical, hypersensitive woman, who was so totally focused on her richly creative inner world, as a mother, and this is understandably an aspect of herself that is completely absent from her writings.

In late 1966 Anna found it necessary once again to vindicate her method in 'The Cold World', confident that she had written a book wholly in keeping with the times. With renewed frustration she attempted to impress on Peter Owen and Philip Inman that her intentions were consciously and diametrically opposed to the realism they continued to look for in the book.

I wish I knew how to make the book more acceptable. When I started writing, I saw the story as one of those recurring dreams (hence the repetitive voyages etc) which at times become nightmare. This dreamlike atmosphere is the essence of the whole concept. Without it, the book would be meaningless. It is an effect very easily damaged or lost altogether, which makes me rather nervous about revision. I wish I could see how this could be done.

In saying that the pursuit is too endless and too drifting, you seem to be objecting to the book as a whole, since the pursuit is the book. The girl's importance as a victim should be enough to justify the pursuing. I mean that peculiar attraction between victim and victimiser, drawing two opposite poles together until finally they are identified with one another. This should become clear through all she says and does, as well as what happens to her, inferred rather than stated directly. I feel direct characterisation would be out of place here and would upset the interpersonal balance between the characters.

When you say you hope for some dramatic incident I am puzzled. I thought the book was full of dramatic incidents with all those fights, shootings, escapes and so on. How could I make the action more pronounced? The book consists of action, doesn't it? I'm not sure what you mean by its internal logic. As I've said, this is not realistic writing. It is meant to be a fantasy or a dream, and dreams are not logical; that's what makes them strange and fascinating (frightening too). To me the characters are very real, so it's hard for me to see why you find them so nebulous and unsatisfactory.

Anna's eloquent defence of the novel she now called 'The Ice World' was highly pertinent, as together with J.G. Ballard she was part of a decade in which inner space and the author's biochemistry, often altered by drugs, became the new dimension for innovative fiction. The idea of a clear distinction between inner and outer realities was dissolved as drugs such as LSD opened out consciousness into hallucinated states that questioned all received notions of reality.

It was not until 28 December 1966 that Peter Owen sent a letter of acceptance, a contract and further suggestions for cuts. Anna now came up with *Ice* as the title she found most effective.

Ice was metaphorically Kavan's heroin white-out, her acknowledgement that her case was terminal and her increased quotient of the drug starting to grow unmanageable, and her landscape reflected the big freeze in her veins. There was certainly no lack of reality in the devastated geography she documented through her imagery for a generation living for the first time under the mushrooming threat of nuclear destruction, as America and Russia competitively tested thermonuclear weapons. Dipping into the political climate of paranoia, Anna intercut the possibilities of hard science with voyages beamed into hallucinated dreamscapes in a novel that harnessed real to imaginary futures.

Ice was Anna's emotional climate and one in which she survived remarkably well. The cold stood for heroin, her family conditioning, the defences she found it necessary to cultivate as a single woman, it stood for withdrawal and the narcosis accompanying attempts at detoxification, it was the clinical white walls of the interior of her flat at Hillsleigh Road with its red fishnet curtains in the bathroom, and it was synonymous with the London winters that she feared on account of her extreme thinness as an addict. It was her natural demeanour until trust allowed her to drop her guard. It was also the cellulose gloss to the paintwork of the fast cars she loved. But, above all, Anna's cool was highly creative, as power-pointed as Sylvia Plath's hysteria and every bit as breathtakingly original.

The visionary landscapes give *Ice* its permanence, a fact not lost on a new generation looking to find in writers such as Anna Kavan the equivalent of chemical states experienced doing drugs. Forty years older than the youth culture coming into prominence, Anna was none the less, like the middle-aged William Burroughs, one of the truest voices of the 1960s in affirming the importance of a literature written without apology for the pharmaceutical input that helped shape its vision. She was, however, more conventional in her form than Burroughs, producing work that was dangerously lucid and concentrated as a blue diamond. Her frozen topology was the equivalent of the cold injected dazzle of Chinese rocks.

I thought of the ice moving across the world, casting its shadow of creeping death. Ice cliffs boomed in my dreams, indescribable explosions thundered and boomed, icebergs crashed, hurled huge boulders into the sky like rockets. Dazzling ice stars bombarded the world with rays which splintered and penetrated the earth, filling earth's core with their deadly coldness, reinforcing the cold of the advancing ice. And always, on the surface, the indestructible ice-mass was moving forward, implacably destroying all life. I felt a fearful sense of pressure and urgency, there was no time to lose, I was wasting time; it was a race between me and the ice. Her albino hair illuminated my dreams, shining brighter than moonlight. I saw the dead moon dance over the icebergs, as it would at the end of our world, while she watched from the tent of her glittering hair.

In tune with the age, Anna had succeeded in creating a metaphysical thriller, a book that eluded the definitions of science-fiction, despite Brian Aldiss voting *Ice* the Best Science Fiction Novel of 1967, and instead pushed those frontiers inwards, looking to inner rather than outer space as the location for a fiction that projected poetic vision into contemporary anxiety. With its lapidary imagery, alien landscapes and lack of geographical signposting, *Ice* was Kavan's vision of a post-human future, the novel that crystallized her private obsessions into a cryo-fiction in which her nameless characters remain frozen like the bodies or preserved heads suspended in liquid nitrogen awaiting resurrection at Alcor.

15

The Loop

*

CONCURRENT WITH WORKING on 'The Cold World' and other fiction projects including extensive drafts for the proposed novels 'Oswald and Rejane' and 'The Words of Mercury Are Harsh After the Songs of Apollo', Anna wrote and completed the quintessentially perfect novella *Who Are You?* in the early 1960s.

André Breton's *Nadja*, perhaps the most innovative and influential text to emerge from surrealism, is probably the book closest to the experimental time-loop and poetic design of *Who Are You?* Breton begins his oblique, obsessive anti-novel with a question of identity that initiates the story of a complex relationship with an unpredictable and unconventional young woman in a manner as compulsive as Anna's update of the theme. Synchronicity plays a major part for both writers in shaping the interaction between characters. Things happen by chance, as they do in life, rather than through the premeditated plot at work in most mainstream fiction.

Although Anna admitted to some literary influences, such as Kafka and Djuna Barnes, and later in life expressed a liking for Jean Rhys's *The Wide Sargasso Sea* and Brian Aldiss's science-fiction novels, as well as the novels of Anthony Powell and Julian Green, she turned more to contemporary French novelists, pioneers of the *nouveau roman* such as Alain Robbe-Grillet, Claude Simon and Marguerite Duras for inspiration, authors published in English translation by the pioneering independent Calder and Boyars.

By the time she came to work on *Who Are You?* writing had not only become Anna's singular reason to exist but also a filter through which to review aspects of her past in the attempt to re-evaluate what continued to disturb. Death was no longer a fact to be endlessly deferred or consigned to an improbable future but a distinct biological possibility for her user's disordered metabolism. It was this and the need to free herself of the shadow it continued to impose on her psyche that had Anna return for subject matter to the imaginative re-creation of the collapse of her first marriage in *Who Are You?*

Like everything she wrote, *Who Are You?* was ahead of its time, a perfectly realized poetic novel in which economy of form is matched by the excruciating tension of the autobiographical contents. It was rejected by Peter Owen because it was too short to stand on its own. Sceptical of its commercial potential, Owen suggested supplementing the novel with a selection of short stories, an idea that did not find favour with its author. Around the same time she submitted another novel, possibly an early draft of *The Parson*, to Peter Owen, who rejected it on the grounds that it was too short to have sales potential. When he revised his opinion and asked to see it again, he was told it had been destroyed, something that seems unlikely given Anna's disciplined method of redrafting work in progress over several years.

Fortunately *Who Are You?* was taken up by the enterprising Scorpion Press, a small publishing house based in Lowestoft, Suffolk, that specialized mainly in poetry. With its attractive lipstick-red design by Laurence Edwards, the image on the jacket reflected not only the hallucinatory quality of Anna's writing but the implosive, drugs-inflected pop art synonymous with the rise of the 1960s' counterculture.

It is tempting to read the narrative of this novella as unreconstructed autobiography, and certainly its intensely claustrophobic, vacuum-sealed account of an inexperienced girl subjected to the arrogant contempt and physical tyranny of an older husband tetchily simmering with paranoid resentment in the tropics reads like a direct re-creation of the psychological trauma that Anna experienced in her marriage to Donald Ferguson. The son in the novel is the product of the girl being violently raped by a whisky-shot, ferociously desensitized husband who forces himself on her with the sole intention of producing an heir. Anxious to subjugate the highly imaginative, independently minded girl to the domestic routine of motherhood and burn the dream-space out of her head, his act of possession is a forcible revenge. The hallucinated, steamy writing carries with it the torrid, heady tang of the tropics, in contrast to the glacial nuclear winter that was the landscape of the other novel she was writing. In *Who Are You?* there is the same invasive totality of landscape as in *Ice*, only it is the solidity of heat and not cold that bears down.

The noise of the frogs fills the night, as the brain-fever birds' cries fill the day. The two sounds are interchangeable in her head, composing one continuous, exasperating background sound, without end or beginning, that finds its way into every single second of the day and night. Not for one of all those seconds has she ever felt at home in this house. She has no clear impression of the darkened country outside; it is to her just a feeling of alien, burning brilliance, heat and confusion, and of mysterious nocturnal cries that burst unaccountably out of solid blackness.

Mr Dog Head is in the novel, as Ferguson appears to have been in life, totally out of sympathy with the girl's intellectual pursuits and her retreat into the world of books to the exclusion of conversation. Like most of Anna's male subjects he is provided with no personalizing name and represents stereotypical machismo of the kind to which Anna seems understandably to have had an aversion. The girl's revulsion for her husband reaches an apogee of loathing that reduces Mr Dog Head to a blank.

She sees that she can't put off talking to him any longer, and reluctantly raises her head, confronting his angry face; it looks to her hard, blank and impenetrable as a wall, with two blue glass circles for eyes above the hard, almost brutal mouth. What possible contact can she have with the owner of such a face? It half frightens her. (After all, she's only just eighteen, and he's double her age.) Feeling bewildered and helpless, she wonders why she's been pushed into marrying him.

The notion of precarious boundaries of identity, a commonly observed symptom of most breakdown sufferers, who either fear or undergo depersonalization, was at the core of Anna's writings. In a recently discovered undated sketchbook that came to light via a house clearance, but which owes its provenance to Raymond Marriott, Anna's recurring motif, written as a caption to accompany most of the drawings, is 'Who When Why'. The drawings are largely variants of an imagined self-portrait, always the one emaciated but aesthetically compelling face with black, spacy dilated eyes staring at no one and nothing, an image to which she persistently returned as though in search of her own identity. The face of the drawings and extensive paintings is a reworked clone, a post-human substitute for the person she never really discovered in any of her various incarnations as Helen Woods, Helen Ferguson, Helen Edmonds or Anna Kavan and who again she went in search of in *Who Are You?* In attempting to visualize ourselves we invariably re-create a subjective image that relies on the psychological type with which we identify. However we come to manipulate the image over the years, we usually situate its characteristics in youth. We look backwards and rarely forwards in re-visioning the self. Most of Anna's drawings and paintings are of a woman fixed in time at the age of twenty-five or thirty. There are no portrayals of herself as an older woman, any more than there are in Francis Bacon's obsessive attempts to reconstruct an excoriating facial image rather than a representative self -portrait.

If Rhys Davies and Raymond Marriott as Anna's executors had not taken it on themselves to morally adjudicate over the subject matter of her paintings and to destroy whatever they considered compromising to her reputation, then the more extreme erotic and mental states she explored through her art, and in the late novels *Who Are You?* and *Ice*, would doubtless have offered further clues as to the nature of her complex sexuality. That Davies and Marriott took offence at sadistic images of figures hanging from their own entrails and in various states of autopsied evisceration was eventually damaging to Anna's reputation as an artist. This aberrant makeover of a woman who lived in her interior world to the exclusion of most forms of reality was of course motivated by the desire to protect her reputation. What Davies and Marriott had not calculated on was that Anna's work would become a cult and that her readers, far from being alienated by the hallucinated, up-ended and often acutely disturbing aspects of her work, would turn to her books precisely to discover these things.

Who Are You? is constructed as a loop. The characters live the same situation twice in a novel that continually questions the nature of being a witness to events by dissolving dream and reality into interdependent states. What actually happens the first time round is remembered differently the second – a highly original experiment on Anna's part – suggesting that how we recollect experience may differ substantially from how things actually happened. What we remember, she implies, is by the nature of memory a fiction. We invent a story in the process of retrieving the facts. Anna's novel exists as the interface between these two questionable states and turns the volume right up on madness in the intense arena of mutual hostilities governing a savagely redundant marriage.

Dog Head's main recreation in the novel is drunkenly bludgeoning rats with a tennis racket, a devastatingly bloody and weird pursuit by most standards, and the girl loathes him for his twisted rages, perversity and pathological violence. Whether in real life Donald Ferguson stalked Burmese rats we will never know.

Like so much of what happened to Anna, the reasons for her leaving her first husband have entered the realm of disinformation.

Her case for the experimental angle of her novel was cogently argued.

I wanted to abandon realistic writing insofar as it describes exclusively events in the physical environment, and to make the reader aware of the different, though just as real, 'reality' which lies just beyond the surface of ordinary life and the surface aspect of things. I am convinced that a vast, exciting new territory is waiting to be explored by the writer in that direction. To explore it, unconventional techniques are required. For instance, the repetition of certain incidents in the same or slightly differing forms is meant to create a three-dimensional effect – an effect in depth – and to show that there is no 'absolute' reality, but that every happening will appear different at different times to different people.

By avoiding any detailed characterisation or plot, I wanted to free the reader from the actual written word, so that he would not be trapped in a piece of reportage, but stimulated to relate what is written to his own and the whole human condition, which of course is again different for each individual.

Like all British writers who abandon social realism for a more adventurous imaginative fiction, Anna was marginalized by a literary mainstream locked into a groove of treating the novel as reportage. If she had been younger in the 1960s, she might well have responded to William Burroughs's junk novel *The Naked Lunch* as a way forward for pharmaceutically metabolized fiction. Burroughs's cut-up technique and assimilation of the argot of the heroin-using underworld revolutionized fiction in a way that few liberated practitioners could avoid. Burroughs effectively blew apart the case for the linearly constructed narrative of the realistic novel, although it continues to be the entrenched form of British fiction today. Anna seems equally to have bypassed the objective cool of Alexander Trocchi's *Cain's Book*, one of the first of the 1960s' novels to make heroin addiction its theme, and to have remained unaware of B.S. Johnson's courageous attempts to rewrite fiction through books such as *Trawl*.

Although *Who Are You?* is free of overt drug references, the angular take on life common to the user is a biological subtext. Anna's desire to create a three-dimensional effect anticipated the 1960s' interest in psychedelia and perception facilitated by hallucinogens such as LSD. Pop art was primarily brokered in

London by Robert Fraser's Gallery at 69 Duke Street, which showed artists such as Andy Warhol, Bridget Riley, Peter Blake and Richard Hamilton, all of whose work fused with a new strain of rock music that set out to interpret the psychoactive experience as part of the psychically expansive epoch in which Anna wrote her best work. Happenings like the famous 14-Hour Technicolor Dream at Alexandra Palace and the strobic 120-decibel light shows introduced by the Pink Floyd to accompany their stage act at the UFO Club in Tottenham Court Road were all part of the collective mind-set with which Anna intersected on an unconscious level in her final decade.

Chance, the design of the moment, the inability to know who we are or what we are doing here, are motif .ken up as a continuous reprise in her novel, nowhere more eloquentl\ ∙∙ essed than in the passage where Mr Suede Boots questions the coincidenc   ..ing to his improbable meeting with the highly introspective girl.

> I wouldn't be here with you now. This wouldn't be real – something else would. You'd have been another you, instead of the one you are now. You can't be tied down to a predestined fate when you change according to your situation, and your fate must change too. Everything depends on circumstances – on which 'you' you happen to be at a given time . . .

The book attracted the renewed attention of Anaïs Nin, whose similar preoccupation with inner landscapes as the source of her fiction had led her to find parallels with her own work in *Asylum Piece* and *Sleep Has His House*. Unable to meet the reclusive Anna, Nin wrote:

> I was very pleased to get your letter and to understand what happened. I have been a loyal friend of your writing for years. I like your last book *Who Are You?* I like the original concept of the twice told story, which is so psychologically true to the variable aspects of reality. Your writing is clearer than ever, while dealing with subtleties, and the images and feelings strong, full of intensity and suspense. It is a unique book. Your strength lies in the skill and clarity with which you describe obscure and mysterious sensations. I always mention *Asylum Piece* as an example of classical lucidity while entering irrational worlds . . .
>
> I resent people's desire to know more about me, when I am in the work, but not from those I feel I can trust. I hope you don't mind my interest. I asked Peter

Owen about you, but as you know better than anyone else, people can only SEE what is like them. In spite of his respect and admiration, he could give me no image of you . . .

    Your book with its condensation should appeal to France. I love the beginning with the birds crying: Who are you? Who are you Anna Kavan? And what a fraud Lawrence Durrell was, promising to look at reality from every angle, and then remaining outside like Pierre Loti, lifting his preface from Proust, but you had the courage to keep your eyes wide open all the time.

    This was not the sort of approach likely to gain favour with Anna or to stimulate her trust, and she later rejected the proposed introduction to *Ice* that Nin provided for Peter Owen. Nin's consistent belief in Anna's subjective explorations, an affinity she shared, seems not to have been reciprocated by the either uninterested or habitually reticent Kavan. But Nin's admiration was genuine, and in her book devoted to the study of the 'poetic novel', *The Novel of the Future*, Nin was to call *Asylum Piece* 'a classic equal to the work of Kafka . . . in which the non-rational human being caught in a web of unreality still struggles to maintain a dialogue with those who cannot understand him'.

    In the way of writers whose work has an ongoing continuity, Anna was busy at the time of the publication of *Who Are You?* with work in progress on 'The Cold World' and the short stories that did not find a publisher until after her death. Nor was her life wholly without pleasure, and the book's publication, coinciding with big autumn rains bringing down green and gold star-shaped plane-leaves in gusts along Holland Park Avenue, was a small occasion to celebrate. By way of a social life Anna regularly visited the Mermaid Theatre and the Salisbury with Raymond Marriott, and the two often had dinner together in Anna's flat, her allowance extending to the regular bottles of gin and wine that Marriott was usually asked to buy on her account. She continued, too, to monitor the local property market, recommending to Rhys Davies that she accompany him to view a number of bachelor flats advertised by Edward Erdman and Co. in a luxury block at the top of Campden Street. She also went with Davies to see Maria Callas perform Donizetti's little-known opera *Poliuto* at La Scala – Callas was afflicted with nerves throughout the performance – and knowing Davies's obsession with the capricious diva Anna saved him whatever Callas clippings she could find.

    Who Are You was favourably received. Anna's difficulty was not a lack of inspiration or creative infertility; it was a matter of finding publishers sympathetic to the new direction her work had taken. This was a problem she had anticipated a decade earlier, writing to Raymond Marriott of the poor reception given *Sleep Has His House*. 'I suppose one must just be resigned to frustration and concentrate on the glittering prizes you speak of – not that I know what they are or where they may be found. Perhaps you'll tell me sometime.'

16

A Woman's Story

*

Anna Kavan had a thing about lipsticks and hoarded over forty different shades of orange, pink and beige to complement her translucent skin. Her thin pencilled eyebrows forming two violet arches in the style of Marlene Dietrich, together with her bottle-blonde hair, gave her the imperious, slightly frosty look of a film star waiting for a leopard-skin upholstered limousine to rescue her from the invasive hassle of real-time living. Anna possessed inimitable style and incorrigible cool. Most comfortably dressed in tastefully chosen slacks and loose jumpers, throughout her life she shopped compulsively for clothes in the hope of having the purchase pleasure compensate for her largely depressed state.

Her friend Rose Knox-Peebles has commented on Anna's confession that the reason she bought so many clothes was that she never dared walk out of a shop without buying anything. Rhys Davies describes her capricious expeditions to big stores to buy a new dress and a gold chain as a desire to immerse herself briefly in mundane reality. She got a sticky high from the sales floors of Barkers in Kensington High Street, Harvey Nichols, Peter Jones or Harrods. In her last years she became almost as reclusive as Garbo, but outwardly the image of unreconstructed glamour never changed. To Rose Knox-Peebles she really did seem in some ways to belong to another species, 'partly because her whole persona, her illness, her drug-taking, her many husbands, etc., didn't fit into the everyday world in which I lived'.

Her agent Bruce Hunter remembers her hospitality on the visits he paid her towards the end of her life and the Martini cocktails with which he was supplied sitting outside in the dense tropical luxuriance of her roof garden elevated in mid-flight between London W8 and W11. Outwardly shy, inwardly Anna was a frustrated romantic, loyal to her ineradicable sense of loss and hurt as a woman while at the same time transcending the emotional damage and burn-out through the continuous stream of her fiction.

Her books are inseparable from a life pursued in the interests of affirming the individual at a time when women were expected to suffer bad marriages without complaint or thought of divorce. Ideologically free of proto-feminism, but artistically committed to independence of mind and spirit for women, as early as the writing of *Let Me Alone* in 1930 Anna identified with solitary creative fulfilment as a prescient destiny, rather than the compromise made by trying to fit with the social contract of marriage. Her epiphanic flash of self-realization in that book had by the 1960s come to sound courageously liberating. 'In a moment everything was made plain to her . . . How easy and simple to face life from the single basis of her own undeniable individuality. She was what she was: herself. No need for compromise or apology or modification or defence.'

Rather like the books she wrote, Anna's beauty was unconventional, matching the image of an intransigent, intellectually liberated woman. She had a quiet, husky voice and spoke in the slow, affected drawl of bleached 1940s' heroines such as Marlene Dietrich and Jean Harlow, as though her vocal chords were furred from cigarette smoke. Rhys Davies's brother Lewis, who knew Anna well in 1945, remembers her speaking voice as 'soft and musical' and possessed of a memorable, inimitable quality.

Anna's obsessive love of clothes extended to sending rejects from her excessive wardrobe to her old school friend Ann Ledbrook, the mother of Rose Knox-Peebles, who as a young woman found herself drawn into the elaborate support system that Anna demanded of her small circle of friends and who would also benefit from the expensive designer throwaways. The friendship between her mother, who was extremely shy, and Anna Kavan seemed an unlikely alliance to Rose, but it was a bond that dated back to Malvern Girls' College, initially cemented by their both having survived the flu epidemic in 1918, which had claimed lives at the college. The clothes would always contain traces of her signature scent – Trésor by Lancôme. Trésor, a complex, fascinating confection of floral notes including lilac, iris, heliotrope, lily of the valley and a hint of violet all sustained by a predominantly sandalwood base, was the perfect Kavan scent. Among the items in the intermittently dispatched clothes parcels Rose Knox-Peebles remembers the excitement of requisitioning a charcoal-grey pair of court shoes with criss-crossed white stitching and Louis heels from the items intended for her mother.

Anna also had a thing about interiors, and her Hillsleigh Road flat was once featured in the Homestyle section of the *Daily Sketch* under the headline 'A Spot of High Class Mind Bending Needs an L-shaped Room', by Edna McKenna: 'Miss Kavan writes strange but enthralling novels in a science fiction framework which excite the respect of other rather highbrow authors.' A complete photo layout of the flat was also published in the *Weekend Telegraph* magazine. Her houses were always bright and light, with white walls, Venetian blinds, modern fixtures and the ingenious use of space to incorporate three-dimensional effects. At Hillsleigh Road her L-shaped top floor contained a mixture of old and new furniture, including a dressing-table with the top drawer crammed with make-up and two large circular mirrors positioned on top of it, the mirrors into which Anna would stare as gateways to vision when writing. In the photograph taken of her at the time of the publication of *Ice* she is seated in a *faux*-leopard-skin-covered lounging chair, her mother's gilded harp prominently featured next to her, and with her Burmese gong coffee table carrying an arrangement of hydrangeas in a vase, most probably cut from her garden. Her bed at Hillsleigh Road was bright red, complete with a canopy. The walls were lined with books, and her paintings in their vibrantly explosive colours were hung on the white walls. The carpets were uniformly white and the upholstery off-white. She made imaginative use of geometric form, offsetting one cube inside another to make an L-shape and divide the living-and-dining room from the kitchen and bedroom, which she justified in the interests of compression: 'Most flats waste a terrible amount of space, with rooms opening off corridors, and doors everywhere. I wanted something that would be very easy to run, so that I could get on with my writing.'

Her obsession with white interiors was aimed in part at a glacial perfection, almost an architectural stab at the Platonic archetypes. 'All the walls in the flat are white,' she told the *Weekend Telegraph*, 'to add a feeling of spaciousness, and the polished parquet floors have off-white Indian rugs.' The gilded harp served as a room divider, separating the dining end from the living area, while the modern credenza carried a globe and an effigy of Rangda, the Burmese witch who abducts children at night. The walls served as a personal gallery showing her own viscerally ethereal creations, and as a reminder of the family she had never really had there was a life-sized portrait of her great-grandmother, Annie Sybella Woods, framed against the searingly beautiful colours of her own compositions and the unharnessed symmetry of meticulously cultivated climbing plants. The top floor of the complex of rooms in which she lived was reached by an outside staircase. Raymond Marriott lived on the floor below in a separate apartment. There was a garage, which was compulsory at the time the building was constructed, and dense foliage in the garden Anna cultivated at the back. The house was in every way the external diagram of her inner preoccupations, its signposting a map of her figurative journey to the interior.

Because she painted a lot in her later years, there were drawers of her intense visionary pictures. Over the years she evolved into a gifted painter whose hallucinated subject matter acted as the visual interface between her dream world and the mutable plasma of her fiction. The paintings created at Hillsleigh Road were largely gouaches, with Anna either dabbing the paint on to the paper with a sponge or filtering it through the interstices of a plastic fruit punnet to create a mosaic effect. Rose Knox-Peebles relates that in the months preceding her death Anna painted a series of suicides, concentrating like Francis Bacon on the forensics of facial impact to create a highly disturbing group of heads attesting to nihilistic despair at the end of things. Marriott and Davies destroyed these paintings in a garden bonfire at Hillsleigh Road.

Anna's readers have had little chance to be exposed to the electrifying dynamic of her surviving paintings because they are either in private ownership or archived together with the bulk of her papers in the McFarlin Library at Tulsa, Oklahoma. Her colours sometimes have the zingy citric tones of lime or orange, or they are derived from steamy jungle greens, blacks that resemble opium paste and blues that seem to have stepped out of a Chinese sea dawn, realized in a way that celebrates a refined aesthetic in conflict with a ubiquitous death-wish. Her paintings, like her writings, are redeemed by an unashamed aura of beauty. Like the neurally convulsive hysteria mapped in the faces that Antonin Artaud drew and painted in his last years of confinement at the Rodez asylum, Kavan's variant depictions of an introverted shattered female archetype are always of a face attached to beauty as an ultimately enduring ideal.

Inveterately impractical, Anna could not change her typewriter ribbons and relied on the man who delivered her small brown wholemeal loaves from Barkers in Kensington High street to change light bulbs and undertake other small domestic tasks. Her cooking was simple and nutritious. She would do grilled trout, a favourite of hers, with a salad dressed with oil and vinegar on the spoon and by way of dessert a fruit compôte with baked custard, all prepared in her minute kitchen. For Raymond Marriott's evenings upstairs she would often prepare veal.

Independent of addiction, failed marriages, breakdowns and a tendency to depression, there was a still darker shadow on Anna's later life that without doubt added to the general despondency she felt in the lonely years following Bluth's death. One of the reasons that Rose Knox-Peebles gives for Anna's not driving, despite her love of fast cars, was that in 1958 she had killed a pedestrian in a car accident. If this was so, then the story 'Fog', in *Julia and the Bazooka*, may well be a fictionalized account of an event that would have added to Anna's psychopathology. In 'Fog' the driver admits: 'I always liked to drive fast. But I wasn't driving as fast as usual that day, partly because it was foggy, but mainly because I felt calmly contented and peaceful, and there was no need to rush. The feeling was injected of course.' The accident as it is described in Anna's story is a model of dissociation. The driver can't make the situation or the danger real.

> Then there was a bump, and I gripped the wheel hard with both hands as if this was what had to be done to avert some disaster – precisely what disaster seemed immaterial. The incident was unduly prolonged. Strange caterwaulings went on interminably and indistinct shapes fell about. When at last it was over, I drove on as if nothing had happened. Nothing had really. I didn't give it a thought, there was nothing to think about. I just went on driving calmly and carefully in the fog, the windshield wipers swinging regularly to and fro, promoting that peaceful dreamlike sense of not being present.

For the dust jacket of *Ice* Peter Owen asked for another photograph besides the much-used one by Walker Evans, and she produced one of herself nude, lying on sand dunes in the South of France, only to have it rejected as unsuitable. She may have been asexual or sexually depressed because of her heroin use but not as a result of moral inhibitions: she supported a radio appeal to endorse the micro-skirt in the mid-1960s, and in her younger pre-contraceptive years seems to have been fully sexually motivated. Francis King and others of her friends assumed that she had lesbian tendencies; there is a hint of this in the Helen Ferguson novels but no other direct evidence. Women who are attracted to gay men for whatever reason, be it the security of freedom from sexual advances or a genuine empathy with same-sex relations, are not necessarily gay themselves. Anna was undoubtedly intrinsically camp, and this would explain her attraction to the likes of Herman Schrijver, Peter Watson, Denham Foutts, George Bullock, Gerald Hamilton, Raymond Marriott and Rhys Davies and also her fondness for visiting the Salisbury pub in St Martin's Lane on the corner of Cecil Court, with its predominantly theatre-going and non-scene gay clientele. It was a safe place for her to dress in the silver evening gown that Francis King remembers her wearing on occasions and to be admired for her frosty glamour, the husky intimacy of her voice and the stylized persona she projected in such company.

Her increasing distaste for sexual relations grew in part out of a profound disillusionment not only with men but with humanity in general. In the story 'The Old Address' from *Julia and the Bazooka*, a fictionalized account of the painful process of detoxification, she writes with misanthropic loathing of a world she had come to find intolerable.

> Why am I locked in this nightmare of violence, isolation and cruelty? Since the universe only exists in my mind, I must have created the place, loathsome, foul as it is. I live alone in my mind, and alone I'm being crushed to suffocation, immured by the walls I have made. It's unbearable. I can't possibly live in this terrible, hideous, revolting creation of mine.

There was no room for relationships in Anna's later solipsistic, drug-managed and painfully solitary existence. Something of her extreme vulnerability is apparent in the fact that when she went into hospital for treatment for her spine, a process in which she would be left for hours lying on a trolley with mauve lines drawn all over her back, she appointed Rose Knox-Peebles her next of kin in the absence of any family of her own.

She reputedly threw a breakfast tray over her first husband in response to one of his drunken rages. Men who identify strictly with their masculinity often feel threatened by a woman's creative dynamic, and it is possible that both Donald Ferguson and Stuart Edmonds were resentful of the imaginative autonomy through which Anna maintained her independence. She did not need men in the conventional sense of wanting to create a family, be financially dependent or emotionally subordinate. She was her own creation at a time when women were expected to endorse the ideology of male superiority. That her trust was irrevocably shattered by the emotional debris of her first marriage and by the devastating consequences of a trail of failed relationships only compounded her vision of life and human relations as essentially nihilistic.

Interviewed by Melvyn Bragg on the *South Bank Show* programme, Francis

Bacon attributed the cause of his creativity to 'being optimistic about nothing'. The same tendency to confront an ontologically based pessimism with an irrepressible creative drive was present in Anna's consistent attempts to overcome the gravitation towards anomie and depression by working. She was as compulsive a writer as Kafka, and independent of her published work she wrote journals that she destroyed in the interest of remaining 'the world's best kept secret', although she did leave behind a vast accumulation of papers and unpublished fragments.

She tended to identify her mother as the principal cause of her traumatized state. The image of the alienated child victimized by a bullying mother intent on suppressing all traits of individuality in her offspring is a common theme in her work and one she drew from life. Rhys Davies has remarked on Anna's self-lacerating perversity bordering on masochism in ostentatiously exhibiting in her flat the portrait of her mother painted by Vladimir Tretchikoff:

> After the death of Anna's mother, an opulent portrait of her hung prominently in the daughter's house. Lavish in oils and idealised execution, its bejewelled subject carried a sheaf of deadly white lilies and a smooth face bore a hostess kind of charm. The painting hung over a dining table on which the daughter wrote her novels and short stories. Visitors could not fail to notice the dominant, if commonplace portrait. Worldly and private success exuded from it. Accustomed to Anna's deepening bitterness towards her mother, to say nothing of her understanding of good painting, I sometimes wondered why she could tolerate the portrait there.
>
> One evening, glaring at it, she attacked its subject with such a depth of hostile repudiation that, accustomed to the sudden minor violence manifested occasionally at this particular hour, I expected a plate or wineglass to be hurled from the dining table: the hour of her evening escape. In her bedroom the palliative would be dissolved in a tiny jar, a syringe – her 'bazooka', she called it – filled, and its needle thrust into a thigh with the efficiency of long, long experience.

In life, as in her books where the victim manifests an inexorable fascination with the oppressor, Anna remained fixated upon her mother's image. Her perverse attraction to the woman she considered her primary antagonist, and as such an indirect link in the biochemical chain leading to her habit, was in part due to her belief that suffering is a necessary part of the creative experience. Her vulnerability was also her strength and, correspondingly, her story.

163

17

Exploding Into Colour:
The Later Paintings

*

ARTISTS WHO APPEAR deeply pessimistic in themselves are often optimistic in expressing that negativity through their art. Anna Kavan's vision in *Ice* celebrates a catastrophic end to the planet through nuclear fission, yet the devastation is redeemed by the imaginative beauty and power of her writing. The same could be said of her painting, which did not fulfil her on the same level as her writing but which she none the less pursued with dynamic vigour and characteristically electrifying *élan* throughout her decade at Hillsleigh Road.

Thanking George Bullock, who had been her occasional secretary, in a letter written around 1966–7, for 'helping preserve these bits of writing that would almost certainly be lost otherwise', she seemed to doubt their ultimate value or merit.

> What their value is I don't know. At the moment I hate the stuff I'm doing now almost more than what I wrote ten years ago. But I guess it is just part of the general lowness. Kth [Bluth] before he left this world was a good estimator of artistic values, and he thought they would find a place among what remains, if anything does.

Her grey state of self-doubt and justifiable hurt at lack of recognition added yet another layer to her impacted depression, yet the paintings that run parallel to her literary creations in the 1960s are characterized by explosive colour in collision with a subject matter that often reflected her distressed inner states. Anna's paintings are, if evidence is needed, still another instance of the creative impulse transcending psychopathology with all the radiant uplift of an orange sun pushing through early morning fog.

She seems never to have signed or dated the intensely beautiful and often violently explosive paintings on which she worked regularly throughout her life. We do know that she exhibited some of them in 1935, at the Wertheim Gallery in London, under the title 'Landscapes in Oil'; but she seems otherwise to have kept her art private, as a facet of herself that she was unwilling to make public. She may well have felt that the difficulties she encountered in later life of interesting publishers in her uncompromisingly innovative genre of fiction would be repeated if she risked trying to secure the representation of a London gallery for her paintings. They carry the same acutely individual signature as her books, their often disturbed, imploded imagery interfacing with the hallucinated content of her fiction. Like J.G. Ballard, Anna is one of the most arrestingly visual of writers, and that she painted with the same intensity as she wrote suggests that she should be taken equally seriously as a painter.

Her legacy as a painter was significantly compromised by the fact that neither of her executors had any great appreciation of her art. After her death Rhys Davies allowed a number of her sympathetic friends and acquaintances, among them Peter Owen, Francis King and Bruce Hunter, to select paintings they would like to have from the assembled repertoire of her later work, and all of these paintings remain in private ownership to this day. Rose Knox-Peebles has three superb gouaches of Anna's – two exceptionally beautiful female heads, their almond-shaped eyes and lubriciously sensual lips hinting at a younger, re-visioned Anna, and a brightly coloured, serenely threatening landscape in which a tiger is about to punch out from a covering of floppy green leaves patterned with a turquoise mosaic.

Anna's paintings, like her novels, depict a self-created rather than an inherited world and are a representation of her individual perception of reality as it is filtered through imaginative sensors. As the result of a house clearance in 2003, a whole cache of Kavan paintings once in the possession of Raymond Marriott have come to light, allowing for an exhibition and a long-overdue appraisal of her work as a painter. Largely work done in the 1960s, they vary between self-portraiture, a broodingly introspective portrait of Dr Bluth with sea-green eyes, imaginary landscapes that have a dreamlike and often sub-aqueous quality, depictions of horses, swans and snakes, a woman's head that has detonated into green foliage, a young Chinaman holding a cat as though conceived in an opium vision, a surreal landscape in which two robotic figures clash while a disdainful girl with a siren's tail looks on, completely unmoved, and outstandingly an androgynous face with hollow black craters for eyes who looks drug-shattered.

To my mind the most compelling of the newly discovered paintings is the schizoid plurality of a young woman with shocking red hair and hugely dilated black eyes who is represented in triptych, each projected figure holding a portrait of herself in a way that powerfully suggests dissociative disorder, a state in which different components of the individual's mind become separated from each other, leading in extreme cases to multiple personalities. This is not to suggest that Anna suffered from dissociative disorder but more that the creative process in her case was capable of empathizing with extreme states often associated with madness. The force of Anna's redhead persona, staring catatonically into the observer's eyes, has the same sort of liberating power as William Blake's depiction of Ahania in 'The Human Harvest' – Ahania in Blake's symbolism corresponding to Ceres. Both figures burn a hole in time by being so absolutely individuated in the present.

Interestingly, one of the newly discovered paintings is the visual complement to the story 'A Visit' from *Julia and the Bazooka*, written in 1965, which begins:

One hot night a leopard came into my room and lay down on the bed beside me
... It was almost too dark to see the lithe, muscular shape coming into my room, treading softly on velvet paws, coming straight to the bed without hesitation, as if perfectly familiar with its position.

In the painting the familiar blonde-haired woman lies asleep, her head resting on her right hand, which in turn is supported by a green and blue jungle floor. The leopard appears completely benign in its expression as it approaches the topless woman, an extended paw placed lightly on her left shoulder. The ocean across which the creature will walk in Anna's story forms a turquoise undulating backdrop. The painting with its oneiric imagery is invested with the alpha rhythms of sleep, and the bonding of the anorexically beautiful girl with the leopard is one of telepathic coitus. We do not know which came first, the painting or the story, but together they achieve a brilliantly realized and mutually interdependent synthesis. 'I promised to write something about K.T. [Bluth],' Anna wrote to her friend Herman Schrijver in 1965, referring to a group of stories that were published after her death in *Julia and the Bazooka*, and each of these separate pieces is about him. Some are written 'straight', others, rather more fantastic, are in the first person, sometimes as if he were the writer, sometimes as if I was. As a whole it's meant to be a sort of love story – a lament for death – and therefore I feel it ought to be published before the other MS [*Ice*] read by Francis King.

At the same time as Anna was compounding her memories of Bluth into fiction, she painted a portrait of him, applying a mosaic effect to his face. Bluth is caught as she must have studied him hundreds of times, unconsciously assimilating his features in the course of their daily meetings and dialogue as friends. He is portrayed as an intense, pensive individual who appears to be either thinking or listening. The prominent forehead suggests someone highly intelligent and predominantly cerebral. The man is all head, and his brain is his motor. The refined nose and thin lips are part of the package. The mosaic patterning him is like the activation of brain cells, a neuronal electricity that drives him as a therapist to sustain a mental framework in which Anna is included. This is not someone who forgets anything Anna wishes him to remember. His alertness in the painting is part of his sensitivity, part of the psychic radar he uses to attune to a patient. Anna has re-created her mentor's intensity in a way that allows us to know how he looked at her and she at him in their peculiar relationship.

There are two fine attempts at self-portraiture in the later paintings in which Anna's cold blue eyes –the colour of February skies – are a prominent feature. The blonde hair, the thinly pencilled eyebrows, the tightly contracted lips and the aura of deep suffering contained in the face all combine to lend a gravity to the features that is entirely consistent with the Anna Kavan we know through her books. This is not a moribund look, but it is backlit through the eyes by inner pain and the suggestion of inconsolable hurt.

Given that Anna was an inveterate parallel-worlder through the topology of inner space, it is not surprising that in her paintings she was attracted to a subaqueous world in which fish and sea monsters rise from the deeps. In one painting three rapaciously open-mouthed green carnivores with shark-like snouts rise up out of the turbulent blue shallows, invaders of a rocky coastline. We cannot see who or what has attracted their ferocity and so the menace is all the more threatening for being without a designated target.

In another painting six fish rise vertically towards an angler's worm, their wide-open staring eyes expressing dumb passivity. Who will be the first to die? the painting seems to ask, as they all strain towards the wriggling bait. The fish are painted in delicate, translucent colours, appearing transparent in the turquoise water; the intrusion of scarlet, hieroglyphic markings on their skin is a pointer to blood and death at the incision of a hook.

An exploding volcano with steaming smoke and molten lava mushrooming from the fumarole is the subject of a powerful landscape painting, grey mountains receding indifferently under a clear sky as the landscape fries with the ejaculation of fuming rock.

There are serene landscapes, too, among the violently apocalyptic. A seascape in which the tiered waves hang in suspended trance could almost be the product of an opium dream – the fragile pinks, tangerines and anthracite of the waves' movement dissolving all recognizable barriers between sea and sky, dream and reality. There are swans sheltering on an island, and the same birds are also seen as a group, snake-headed and preening on a pond. There is an orchard of shocking yellow mimosa, so exuberantly abundant it forms a dense cloud, and there is a roan foal standing beneath the inquisitive grey head and legs of its mother in a landscape the ferric red of Mars.

There is one late painting in particular that demands total attention on account of its black-out, death-informed underworld connotations. The atrophied, genderless face, the eyes sunk so deeply into black craters that they look like dark glasses, the down-turned mouth both perversely erotic and ruined, are angled on to a grey, bony left shoulder in a posture signalling terminal addiction. The short blond hair and laid back attitude of the addict in a black-walled room creates something of a likeness to Andy Warhol or to the emaciated, peroxided Lou Reed in his *Sally Can't Dance* incarnation, circa 1974. A stormy red sun is windowed on a turbulent, smoky-blue sky. The character in the painting, dead to the world, is none the less anxious, disquieted by involvement with a drug that carries the user to the bottom. This is a junkie with nerves panicked into self-reflection but too pharmaceutically compromised to react. The painting is so powerful that it stares you into submission. On the street this person would weigh six stone and be skewed by the daylight. Kavan only gives us the head and shoulders and leaves the gender to the imagination. The facial assertion is as forceful as a Munch or Bacon, the features every bit as catastrophic. This is someone who lives garaged in a private underworld, a drug-compromised Dorian Gray, a mutant involved in transgendering the species and by their genes irrevocably born to lose. The painting explores a state that Anna must have known first hand, particularly when in her last years and in ill health she was forced to attend the drug dependency clinic at Charing Cross and wait on hard chairs in rooms full of addicts. It is tempting to suppose that Anna had seen such a person in the waiting-room of the clinic and fused their identity to her image of herself as inexorably dependent.

A naked man with a knife through his back kneels on all fours, as though the sexual act has turned to murder. The blade of the knife is buried up to the hilt in his spine and the tip protrudes from his stomach, points up the thematic concerns in her work that so upset her two executors. The red-haired man is another of Anna's imagined an гynes, the body thin as she thought herself thin. There are no cl⸱⸳ 1 the painting as to who is responsible for the atrocity or whether it was ᴗᴗd in the interest of heightening sexual kicks. The landscape framing the man appears to be a bare winter forest with an arched wooden bridge slung across an icy blue stream. The isolation of the place is unrelieved, and the taut, agonized figure, occupying the entire foreground, has either been left in that posture to die or is being watched from behind by her unidentified killer. Both the body and the knife are unstained. There is no stab wound, and we are led to believe that the victim's body is bloodless and that she has the post-biological body of an alien. The murder, it seems, has been as cold and clean as the knife.

In a drawing that could serve as the companion piece to the knifed woman, a full-breasted woman, legs wide open, sprawls abandoned on a *chaise-longue*. Her left hand cups her right breast, while a young girl, her short skirt hitched above her thighs, crawls across the floor towards a chair. Her head is averted to the left as she looks at the older woman's pubis. The scene portrayed hints at something both furtive and illicit. The sex that is suggested has been between an adult and a minor, and the older woman's sated expression implies that her partner has been corrupted or is groomed in the role of compliancy. There is a flask and a shot-sized glass on a small table beside the *chaise-longue*, and the woman snakes her right leg down to the floor while her left leg is angled towards and supported by the low table.

In another painting a solitary figure is being pursued across a clifftop by what looks like a trail of white lava. A male figure jockeys like a skier on a slope, arms thrown out for balance as though the white substance pursuing him is slippery underfoot. Facing him, although his head is turned in the opposite direction, is a white arrow pointing to the drop. The predicament is one of controlled panic.

There is no help anywhere and no way out of the situation. The landscape is empty. The signposting is one way and one way only, and both the man and the trail of viscous white lava pursuing him are headed that way. The muted colours of the landscape, green, white and blue, are unthreatening in themselves, making the action appear all the more terrible in its desperate urgency.

A skeletal angel that could be Luz from 'The Cold World' stands, wings extended, one shapely long leg crossed over the other, on a surface made lapidary by ice. Her extreme thinness, corresponding as it does to Anna's idea of the female archetype, is none the less sexualized by full breasts and defined curves. In this respect the angel in the painting personifies Luz in *Mercury*, who is also the glass girl in *Ice*, an elusive, almost incorporeal figure who is pursued for her sexual allure. Inhuman as she appears, the face wears deep worry-lines, and the white mane of hair streams almost vertically from the head. The girl's left breast is shaped like a lemon, the nipple displaced from the centre to a sideways-pointing nozzle. She is odd, alienated and, like most of Anna's characters, inhabits a solitary, alternative universe.

A figure is being hunted on a quarry floor, his exhausted white body about to capitulate to the blow of a heavy stick. We do not know what has brought the three figures there, only that the third is attempting to restrain the aggressor. The action takes place under a vertical grey quarry face, a rift of blue sky showing above, the three figures appearing freeze-framed in their acute isolation. The influence of Kafka on Anna's writings is apparent in the theme of this picture with its emphasis on the portrayal of the inhuman justice that is so often a part of life.

In another painting an unidentifiable creature which could be an alien, an extraterrestrial or a light-form wings it above aquamarine water, sleek pink skin resembling latex, the humanoid face reminding us of reports of common greys in the literature of ufology, only this one lacks the black wraparound eyes usually associated with this species. This is clearly one of Anna's creatures of inner space, the curved keyhole-shaped tail and jaw fissured incisively for the entire length of the face like a zip, giving it the look of a predator. As an admirer of the science-fiction aspects of her work Brian Aldiss would doubtless have approved of Anna's imaging a post-human species in a painting that psychs directly into the alien as a form programmed into and projected by the human psyche.

Her paintings explore themes in common with her fiction in transforming the flipside of life into something beautiful. She was somebody who, by her own admission, needed to look at the sky several times a day in order to find relief in its constantly mutating colours and in the spatial dimension it offered to her ubiquitous interior existence. She never makes dark matter in her work darker but always lifts it poetically into the light, transforming it in the process into a visually retrievable beauty.

Imaginatively uncompromising artists like Anna Kavan stand out in ways that very often attract hostility from their contemporaries. Being individual leads to a sense of over-conspicuousness, a breaking out of conventional moulds that threatens orthodoxy. The mainstream answer to such individuals is either to ignore the work or to denigrate it. Neglecting it is the most effective strategy, although ultimately suppressed work of genuine merit leaks through to be taken up by a cult. In this respect it is consoling to know that Anna Kavan's reputation, like that of Denton Welch, another rogue British novelist who is similarly rediscovered by each new generation of readers on the trail of the dispossessed, has survived with little promotion through the enduring legacy of the work.

Her art is powerfully disturbing in the visceral way of Munch, Soutine and Bacon. We lack any admission on her part as to artistic influences. From some of the female faces in her figurative paintings, she clearly owes a debt to Modigliani in the narrow elongated faces with their Egyptian eyes that are a recurring motif in her work, and there is also a hint of Rousseau in the introduction of tigers and leopards into the exotic jungle of an urban garden. As with her writing she was a one-off, an untutored genius following no other road map but the one of her making. She painted regularly in the L-shaped room at Hillsleigh Road, against the backdrop of her clinically white walls, and cared enough for her work to hang some of her intense, hallucinatory paintings in that cubist space, palpable excerpts from the obsessive inner world she occupied and a manifestation of the tonic colour and flair that were always part of her continuously creative life.

18

The Needle and the Damage Done

*

T HE PUBLICATION OF *Ice* in 1967 helped
considerably to rehabilitate Anna Kavan's literary reputation. After decades of
critical neglect familiar to artists who are considered to have passed their peak, in
her last years she finally intersected with an audience receptive to how she saw
the world.

She had made it to this place late in life and in ill health. She and Raymond
Marriott continued to write to each other three or four times a week, although
they were only separated by a floor, finding in letters a deeper level of communi-
cation. They were generous with each other in exchanging gifts, she buying him
a bright new shopping bag from Barkers and regular bottles of vermouth, and on
29 March 1967 she wrote to thank him for a gift. 'Thank you so much for the
bracelet. I was given one the other day so now I'm fêted. What does one do with
a lot of these – luxuriate, I suppose?' Marriott also helped Anna with the garden,
fetched her bread from Gawes, ironed her scarves, supplied her with free theatre
tickets he received in his capacity as the editor of *The Stage* and was a model
tenant, but more than that he recognized her unique talent as a writer and had an
undying affection for both her and the extraordinary imagination that informed
her work.

As part of her rediscovery, Anna was featured in the September 1967 edition
of *Nova* by the Indian-born poet Dom Moraes. The interview, which began at her
flat and shifted to the Chanterelle restaurant in South Kensington, found her in a
pensive, uncommunicative mood, and her publisher Peter Owen was left to do
most of the talking. From the tone of the article it is clear that Anna took an
instant dislike to Moraes, fixing her distracted attention instead on her mother's
gilded harp and making largely inaudible comments. During lunch at the
Chanterelle, two hours later, she remarked: 'I haven't felt anything for twenty

years.' She expressed her contempt for Moraes by returning the photographer's contact sheets 'marked up in orange lipstick', indicating the one she liked with a bold stroke. Moraes claimed, 'I had to peel the contact sheets apart like onion skins.'

For Anna, as for Jean Rhys who was profiled in the same edition of *Nova*, rediscovery had come too late to be meaningful or attached to any long-term ideas for the future. With Bluth dead and her body showing an increasingly dangerous tolerance to heroin, Anna's life became an exacting round of hospital visits punctuated by periods of recuperation in which she continued to work. Something of her state can be assessed by the fact that she fastened together a number of short stories she intended showing Peter Owen with hypodermic needles.

Brian Aldiss, who visited her at Hillsleigh Road soon after the publication of *Ice*, discovered 'a friendly and welcoming individual' who showed him over her house with a walking stick. In 'Kafka's Sister', his introduction to a selection of her writings called *My Madness*, published by Picador, Aldiss recalled:

> Anna had some complaint about Cyril Connolly, the editor of *Horizon* for whom she had worked in the war years. He could have been more supportive of her with regard to her own writing, she felt. It was the sort of remark anyone might make. She longed to have a reputation, and thought that my attention marked a new start; she liked the idea of being regarded as a science fiction writer. It sounded modern. One sees in her work the sort of modernism – love of cars and speed and so on, not to mention the 'fast set' that surface in Aldous Huxley's novels.

As a result of this meeting Aldiss was later instrumental in getting *Ice* accepted for American publication by his science-fiction editor at Doubleday.

She was also understandably perturbed by having the government monitor her habit and confused and frightened over how she would obtain supplies if she was officially denied the drug. Writing to Raymond Marriott on 29 November 1968, she gave voice to her underlying panic. 'Thank you so much for the needles. I'm sorry you had so much trouble finding them. The entire supply and demand business has gone mad regarding drugs and anything connected with them. It's a conspiracy of course. Oppenheim's at the back of it all.'

A careless injection early in March 1968 resulted in still another infection stemming from a badly abscessed leg. She was admitted to St Charles Hospital, and from there wrote to her friend Herman Schrijver:

> They told me today that I'd probably have to be here two or three weeks longer – a dismal prospect indeed. I only escape a continuous intravenous drip because that might spread the infection. No luxury such as a telephone, and I'm forbidden to use my radio. The food is utterly repulsive and uneatable. I live on sandwiches brought by kind friends!

She was simultaneously being treated as an outpatient for a genetic spinal disorder at the Royal Marsden Hospital. Rose Knox-Peebles supplied transport and psychological support.

Anna felt fundamentally betrayed by Dr Bluth's death and spoke to friends of how she had been 'sold down the river'. She remained adamant that the two had agreed on a suicide pact, in the way that Virginia and Leonard Woolf, fearing Hitler's invasion of England, had acquired against that contingency a lethal dose of morphine for the two of them from Virginia's brother Adrian. Not that her relations with Bluth had ever been easy, least of all when they involved company. Shortly before Bluth died Anna had found it necessary to apologize to Raymond Marriott for Bluth's unorthodox behaviour. 'Of course you didn't overstay your welcome. I'm sorry I was so tactless and abrupt. I thought you knew the situation with KT. 99 times out of the 100 it's impossible to have a normal evening with him.' Or perhaps, Raymond would have commented, with Anna.

Life without Bluth was, as Anna had always anticipated, nearly impossible. A whole private world of shared references had disappeared with him, leaving her excruciatingly aware that she now lacked a witness to her life. Acutely vulnerable, she retreated into the world of imagination, like an astronaut doing moon landings in her head, feeling depersonalized, misidentified and special to no one. She promised Marriott that if he could find it in himself to spend more time with her she would do her best 'to behave normally'. But neither Marriott nor Davies was a substitute for Bluth, their chief recommendation being that as gays in an age that criminalized homosexuality they qualified like her as outsiders in the normal society that Anna had progressively outgrown. She found it necessary now to readopt the image of implacable scrutiny and detachment that she had worked so hard on cultivating during her years of nomadic travel in the early 1940s. The diamond severity that could outwardly remain intimidating or hostile was of course a façade created to appear independent and without emotional needs. She was at pains to explain her occasional frostiness to Marriott. 'After you'd gone last night it occurred to me that I might well appear extremely ungracious at times, owing to a certain manner deliberately cultivated years ago (and now automatic) which was meant to give an impression of the toughness I don't possess.'

Marriott, who had published a novel, *The Blazing Tower*, with the Quadrant Press, continued to send Anna his poems on a regular basis for comment. While aware that he possessed a small gift, she was none the less cautious in her praise, reminding him that writing was to her a way of life and not a distraction from it.

> Thanks for the poem. Probably you've forgotten the question you asked, but as it's important, I'll answer anyhow. KT always said you had some creative gift. I think so too. I also think that you don't work nearly enough. What energy you have left after earning your living appears to me to go in far too many directions. A good writer must be simple minded.

She had other problems besides her treatment for an abscessed leg and her escalating use of heroin. A book of short stories had been submitted through her literary agent, David Higham, to Peter Owen and turned down, because Owen felt that only half of the book represented her at her best. He encouraged her to write more and resubmit. Anna feared that the editorial scenario of 'The Cold World' was about to be repeated; she had an abundance of new material, much of which would go into the posthumously published *Julia and the Bazooka*, and somewhat reluctantly agreed to revise in order to meet Owen's demand. She came back to him quickly, perhaps sensing that time was running out.

> I am sending you twenty stories and hope you will find enough material to make up a book. Five you've already seen. I've put them together in the file. I think I told you that I'm doing an autobiography in the form of short stories with a connecting thread (something like *Asylum Piece* and *The House of Sleep* [sic]). But I'd rather keep these separate from the present series, although they are complete in themselves . . . I must apologise too for not answering your letter and kind invitation sooner. I hope very much to come to the party, but could we leave it open, as I still have to go for hospital treatment most days and don't like to commit myself definitely.

The party, thrown at Owen's house in Kenway Road, was to honour Anaïs Nin and the publication of a new volume of her journals. It is unlikely that Anna had any intention of going, still less did she wish to meet Nin, whose introduction to *Ice* she had summarily rejected the previous year.

On the day of the party, 5 December 1968, at the instigation of Raymond Marriott and Rhys Davies the police were called to Hillsleigh Road to break down the door of Anna's flat. They found her fully dressed, sprawled across the bed, a syringe in her arm and her head resting on the lacquered box in which she stored her heroin. She had been dead for twenty-four hours. She had died private and elegant to the last, fully made up, preparing a shot, true to her image of herself and her inner vision right to the end.

Scotland Yard's Drug Squad subsequently thanked Marriott and Davies for informing them of Anna's compulsion to stockpile heroin and discovered in their search of the flat 'enough heroin to kill the whole street'.

19
Disinformation

*

NNA KAVAN WANTED to remain 'the world's best-kept secret', to elude biography and the chronological factoring of events into an approximately re-created life. Facts do not tell a life; they are always subordinate to the complex emotions underlying their existence. The problem with conventional biography is that it uses fixatives in the way liquid nitrogen is used as the preservative in cryogenics. If the subject is dead they are dumb, and so there is no verification of what is written. Biography in that sense is like an autopsy. The data analysed lacks any feedback or dialogue with the living person.

When Anna died on 4 December 1968, putatively of fatty myocardial degeneration, she had been preparing a shot of heroin from the Chinese lacquered box in which she kept her daily supply. The liquid was still in the barrel of the syringe and the plunger had not been depressed. That she collapsed with the needle in her arm after a lifetime's addiction to heroin was sufficient in itself to generate a cult following. The question whether she died naturally or of an overdose has never been settled, given her long history of attempted suicide and her propensity as a serious user to overdose.

As with Sylvia Plath the nature of Anna Kavan's death contributed greatly to her becoming an underground cult. The publication of her last novel, *Ice*, had begun the process of re-evaluation, and the renewed interest in her work was given increased momentum by the publication of two posthumous collections of stories, *Julia and the Bazooka* (1970) and *My Soul in China* (1975), as well as by the issue in paperback of *Asylum Piece*, *Ice* and *Sleep Has His House* by Picador in the 1970s, editions that kicked Kavan's work into the awareness of a receptive post-psychedelic youth generation. In the same decade Peter Owen began a programme of systematically republishing all her major books. The posthumous publication of two additional novels, *Mercury* (1994) and *The Parson* (1995), both retrieved from the Kavan papers at the McFarlin Library at the University of Tulsa, has further consolidated her reputation as one of the great uncompromising originals.

But at what price? Isolation most often breeds suspicion if not contempt in the power structure of the arts, and those who go it alone without recourse to networking and who are set apart by their experiences of mental breakdown or same-sex orientation, are usually at a disadvantage. Anna was sufficiently different to qualify as an outsider. The house in Hillsleigh Road, impenetrable to the outside world and built like the wing of a small medieval fortress, balustrades stretching into the low-flying Kensington cloud, was the extension of Anna's later inscrutable façade and her need to shut out and selectively rewrite reality.

Her psychiatric history remains speculative. Like most obsessives she feared madness but was not mad. Her writing suggests she was visited by the disturbing visual imagery associated with psychotic phenomena, but she was not psychotic. There is no evidence of the multiple personalities or delusional states sometimes manifested in paranoid schizophrenia. Her depression was not clinical in the sense that it left her incapable of functioning. On the contrary, she wrote regularly every day not only as a means of containing her symptoms but as a discipline necessary to her creativity. Depression and anxiety are often symbiotic states, and Anna's use of heroin as a palliative was perhaps a safety behaviour aimed in part at reaction-maintenance, suppressing fears she felt unable to confront. Heroin was a means of avoiding the issue, in the way that an agoraphobic person stays at home rather than risk panicking in Oxford Street. There is clear evidence in her letters and writings that Anna lived with an oppressive sense of dysphoria and that her negative mood was a constant. Most of us experience depression at some time and the factors determining how quickly we bounce back from descent into negativity may have something to do with the distinction between those who react to dysphoria with extreme distress and those of us who do not. It may have been that Anna's coping strategy – heroin – increased her pessimism, leading to the persistence rather than the alleviation of her anxiety. Although she was not passive in the face of psychological stress, heroin is a passive drug in the sense of being a powerful suppressant, and this, combined with Anna's damaged self-esteem and extreme vulnerability, may have increased the duration of her pessimism. Each time she depressed the plunger of the syringe for an attempted dopamine rush, she was paradoxically harnessing her depression to its source. It was inversely part of her addict's frustration: she needed the drug even though its chemical profile kept a lid on her depression. And this perhaps was a form of madness, the establishment of a neurochemical loop by the need to keep repeating an unbreakable habit for forty years. She was not pathologically mad. Rather, she was someone whose extreme sensitivity made her vulnerable to depression and whose imagination set her at an angle to the world of functional materialism.

Brian Aldiss's remark on visiting Anna shortly before her death, that she longed to have a reputation, is telling in that withdrawal from the world is sometimes a process initiated by disappointment. She was not, however, without critical acclaim, and had been noted by the *Weekend Telegraph* as belonging 'in the tradition of the great writers on drug addiction, De Quincey, Wilkie Collins and Coleridge' and had been rightly called 'a remarkable poetic writer who could transmute the most ordinary matter of daily life into a dangerous, haunting vision'. Her prototype in brokering disinformation, the Comte de Lautréamont, succeeded in airbrushing out almost every biographical clue to his existence in Paris at the time of writing his surreal masterpiece *Maldoror*. The indifferent reception given his privately published, viscerally obscene book, in which surrealist imagery combines with extreme anarchy, no doubt prompted his death in a hotel room under mysterious circumstances at the age of twenty-four in 1871. The speculative myth arising from his death (suicide is the most commonly advanced cause) has ensured him not only the regular upgrade of a strictly posthumous reputation but a place in the history of those who by the unspecified nature of their death seem never to have properly died. It is the nature of the living not to let the dead go. In our desire to refresh the significance of our cultural icons who died as unconventionally as they lived, we weave legends around them. We reinvent the likes of Marilyn Monroe, James Dean, Elvis Presley, Sylvia Plath, Jim Morrison, Jimi Hendrix, Kurt Cobain and Anna Kavan and reincorporate them into the living.

Anna was sufficiently a stranger on earth never to give her date of birth. She had no wish to be identified by facts and would doubtless have rejected biography as an invasive tool undermining her privacy. There are writers who live with the idea of being rediscovered after they die as a compensation for neglect; but I doubt Anna would have found consolation in the prospect of her work living on without her awareness of its survival. Posthumous honours do nothing to redress the neglect usually imposed on visionary artists by the reductive politics of their contemporaries. Anna did not network or play the game because she had something better to do – write. She believed, as her sort of sensibility does, that the work should speak for itself, and in an ideal world it would. Instead, she became increasingly neglected over the years to the extent of being almost forgotten by the time Peter Owen became aware of her work in 1957 and began the slow process of rehabilitating her.

To Aldiss Anna's isolation as a writer had a lot to do with her adoption of a predominantly European mode of symbolism as an expression for the novel. She is not in the least concerned with the social resolution of her characters or in their formulaic development within the novel. Her abstract characters, often denied names and simply designated by an initial, do not have a past. Their precinct is the present, and they filter all experience subjectively. According to Aldiss:

> If one plays the game of categories, then Anna Kavan ranks as a symbolist, one of the few English symbolists. It is a rare breed, which is perhaps why she has found no protagonist to speak up for her. A slightly coterie publisher published and nourished her. She formed no alliances with other authors. Her name does not appear in the *Oxford Companion to English Literature*. Symbolism is not a part of the solid English mainstream of writing. We prefer our fictional protagonists to turn into successes or failures rather than leopards.

But for all her exclusion from mainstream consideration Anna Kavan's work has obstinately outlived her for almost forty years, and most of her books are kept in print by Peter Owen. The irony would not have been lost on her that at the Vinyl and Book Exchange bookshop on Pembridge Road, a ten-minute walk from her house in Hillsleigh Road, her books are filed in the prestigious Cult section, as distinct from the rat pack of popular novelists, designated Chickens' Arses. When I was last at the shop a blonde, spiky-haired Japanese cyberpunk was browsing through a copy of the Peter Owen Modern Classics edition of *Sleep Has His House*. The mutant appearance of this young Asian girl turned Aryan, together with the evening sunlight bleeding into the manic rush-hour crowds outside, combined to create a cameo that could have been excerpted from the novel the girl was buying.

The search for Anna Kavan leads inevitably to a disinforming event horizon. Outside of the data stored in her archival assemblages at the McFarlin Library at

Tulsa and the Humanities Research Center at the University of Texas, outside of David Callard's investigative biography, *The Case of Anna Kavan*, and Priscilla Dorr's doctoral dissertation, 'Anna Kavan: A Critical Introduction', the trail of letters and paintings dispersed to private individuals ends abruptly. Anna Kavan is as much a secret as the big sparklers stashed in a Swiss bank vault.

Her work is admired for the intensity of its vision by novelists as different as J.G. Ballard and Doris Lessing, and her niche in cult literature is secure. Being a cult figure is arguably more attractive in terms of enduring mystique and cutting-edge credibility than being commodified into mainstream acceptance. Anna did her own thing independent of prevailing trends, realizing perhaps that the future would be kinder to her than her contemporaries. The appeal of most popular writing is that it looks backwards – it is easier to imitate the past than it is to imagine the future, and in the last of her *Horizon* reviews, 'Back to Victoria', Anna discussed precisely this bias. 'It almost appears,' she wrote, 'as if any popular art-form must, if it is to succeed, have a non-contemporary atmosphere.' Developing her theme that the British obsession with Victorianism was a psychological regression to infantilism, she associated the matter-of-fact terminology of the Victorian novel with the concrete expression of its revivalists. Speaking very much of her own predicament in creating out of the present, she wrote:

> Thus, the isolation of the mature individual becomes greater than ever. For, broadly speaking, all who in their uncertainty abandon the hard abstraction of thought in order to fall back on the prop of concretism; all who write books in this vein as well as those who read them, belong to the ranks of the modern Victorians. Their society, based on the absolute and exclusive power of wealth, has aptly taken a return to the gold standard as a symbol of its material origin. The escapist members of this not brave, not new, order have indeed returned to the ideology of the nursery. Afraid of the vast indifferent world, they cling to the familiar safety of everyday objects; houses, chairs, beds: things that comfort the mind as they support the body.

Her concern with 'the hard abstraction of thought' as the base line to a creativity stemming from the global catastrophe of war wired her to the present as the modality from which she operated. The courage needed to create from contemporary events, lifting them into alignment with the possibility of nuclear wipe-outs and the weaponized eschatologies of the future, was an attribute she recognized in Kafka and Gogol as forerunners of her method, and she used both to advantage in her swipe at the Victorians. She compounds her own beliefs in literature into an aesthetic at the expense of the commonplace issues cementing the Victorians to their advocates in her generation, something that brings her to the mention of Kafka as the most singularly important influence on her work. What concerns her most is Kafka's investment in confronting every aspect of reality, no matter how terrible, and converting it into the subject of art.

> Writers of the quality of Kafka and Gogol do not run away from reality. They have too much integrity, both as artists and human beings, to indulge in escapist flights. Especially sensitive, they are especially vulnerable, and they escape nothing. When life frightens and hurts them, they do not look back at the nursery windows with longing eyes, but incorporate in themselves a part of life's fear and pain. The artistic value of their work endures because it is also part of reality. It is conscious, uncompromising, personal, true. It is life. It is everything the new Victorian tries to avoid.

Anna herself was especially sensitive, especially vulnerable and intent on escaping nothing. Her strength lay precisely in her difference. The Anna Kavan who cashed her heroin prescriptions at Notting Hill Gate and Kensington pharmacies was aware of the fundamental weakness and disintegrity coded into those who lived by the accepted rules of society. Even the *Horizon* crowd, Anna's main contacts in the literary world, were sceptical of her. Arthur Koestler, who was interested in both her work and her mental states, once reproached Cyril Connolly for retailing 'after-dinner stories in which you told with gusto about her last suicide attempt, etc.'. Kavan was gossip to Connolly, a far inferior writer and dilettante, but she was revered by her gay coterie, the men she attracted to her – including Peter Watson, George Bullock, Gerald Hamilton, Charles Schriver, Rhys Davies, Raymond Marriott, her stepfather Hugh Tevis and so many others – who perhaps out of their own personal suffering recognized in Anna a corresponding sympathy, a reciprocal defiance in celebrating what it means to be picked on for being different. Anna was adept at holding her own in the bitchy repertoire of repartee and once told Peter Owen, who had remarked on a snake bracelet she was wearing at dinner, in a suitably insidious voice, 'I love serpents.'

Anna Kavan's reputation as a cult artist was strictly posthumous. She died before the news could reach her that the American publisher Doubleday, who had dropped *Sleep Has His House*, had at Brian Aldiss's instigation, and with the backing of his editor there, Lawrence P. Ashmead, accepted *Ice* for American publication. Anna had written to Aldiss only weeks before the delayed news. 'Sorry this is such a disjointed note. I really don't feel human at present.'

Nobody can retrace the movements leading to what looked like Anna's last failed attempt to inject. David Callard has accepted fatty myocardial degeneration as the cause of Anna's death, although there is no evidence that toxicology screening was a part of the post-mortem examination. Anna had attempted suicide so often in circumstances similar to these that the possibility of an overdose cannot be ruled out. We do know that, feeling an additional need for palliation, she had recklessly increased her quotient of heroin after Bluth's death, and there were likely to be substantial deposits of the drug in her body at the time of her death. She died trying to get herself normal as part of the inexorable pact she had made with a chemical loop so far back that she could no longer remember why she had taken the drug; only that it had reprogrammed her to keep anticipating its high. There is a drawing by Anna in a recently recovered sketchbook of a number of naively executed female figures, under which she has written the caption: 'Give the old people drugs.' The sketch is wilfully subversive and hints at a side of Anna other than the passive junkie – the rebel beneath the composed exterior, the person who was too old to benefit directly from the liberating social changes brought in by the 1960s but whose sympathies were written into the subtext of its youthful rebellion. Anna even called one of her late stories 'Yellow Submarine' as a pointer not only to the Beatles but to the invasive tsunami of psychedelic extravaganza pervading the ethos. In her story 'Tiny Thing' she picked up on Biba, Bus Stop and Carnaby Street, which were the hotspots for 1960s' fashion, and Tiny Thing, the protagonist of the story, 'is a tall fellow with long black hair, wearing a fantastic flowered jacket'. In the story Anna's fictional persona comes across a young man in a nightclub dressed in clothes from I Was Lord Kitchener's Valet:

> As if mesmerised, she stared at his pale face, framed by side-burns and fluffy brown hair, and at his jacket which had been part of an obsolete military uniform resplendent with gold epaulettes and scrolls of gold braid. Although she was perfectly used to eccentric dress, she couldn't help thinking of him as an actor, dressed for a special part; an impression extending to his smile and voice,

which had an East End accent, incompletely disguised by upper-class smoothness.

It was precisely the ability to make a fiction contemporaneous with the changes in her life that led to *Ice* as the summit of her creative achievements. There is little separation between Anna's characteristics as a person in later life and those of the white-haired, androgynously thin female protagonist of *Ice*. In the end she had become her own fiction, rather than its objective creator. The girl in *Ice* was who she inwardly imagined herself to be. Someone alien, inhabiting a virtual body, her skin tone translucent, her sensory communications extraterrestrial, her identity that of a stranger on earth.

In *Trillion Year Spree* Brian Aldiss paid homage not only to *Ice* but to the Kavan myth as it has been perpetuated over the decades.

Anna Kavan's story has been told already – how she too was monstrous, how she had the heroin habit for several decades and came to terms with it, and how she committed suicide one week before the news arrived of *Ice*'s acceptance by Doubleday. The story of *Ice* in many ways bodies forth Kavan's inner life. It is the ultimate in catastrophe – the advance of the ice is real enough but it is also the ice of the soul, the heroin encroaching, the habit of death you can't kick.

MDMA – or ecstacy – is perhaps the chemical for the digital age, but heroin carried a death-bound mystique in the 1960s, far different to the clubby pharmacopoeia of psychotropics available to recreational users today. It was dodgy, expensive and associated with death. Only terminal cases used a needle – the next stop after queuing outside Boots was death. Anna's involvement with heroin on a very private level has fascinated her cult and driven others away. Her work is not to be found in anthologies of drug literature because she did not make drugs the subject of her books, as Burroughs did, or in any way sensationalize her addiction. Instead the drug shaped her writing by what can only be termed substance osmosis. *Ice* is a whitescape heroin novel that never names the drug.

The world of British literature, with its formal resistance to imaginative flair, is prepared to tolerate eccentrics but largely abjures drug users, homosexuals, science-fiction and cyberpunk practitioners. De Quincey and Coleridge can be forgiven their laudanum addictions because they have been metabolized into mainstream literature. Oscar Wilde has been rehabilitated a century after his death because his overriding popularity and eminent quotability have made him indispensable to the media. Anna Kavan has received no such sanction. She continues to remain marginal, cultishly niched and awaiting rediscovery.

I am fascinated by Anna's last moments. What was she wearing at the time, how was she feeling as she went from the clinical environment of her bathroom into the bedroom? None of her letters records cardiac symptoms or a diagnosis of heart problems, at a time when she was attending hospital almost on a daily basis. Should not someone in her medical team have picked up on her condition? Her last act was directed at the brain's reward systems and its pleasure centres in the hypothalamus. At a level of molecular adjustment she had travelled this neural highway most of her life and was an adept at tuning in to the fine details of neurotransmission and chemical synthesis. Flooding the brain with dopamine was her habit, setting into motion second-messenger effects that are known to inhibit the synthesis of certain proteins within cells. She may have been aware that her previous shot was a transcription of a negative mood that had failed to shift and that an adjustment was necessary. She does not seem to have been working on a new novel at the time, although there is no means of dating when in the 1960s she wrote *The Parson*, a short novel that has themes and a stateless geography in common with *Ice*. She certainly seems to have been engaged in writing short stories and preparing final drafts of the twenty she had promised Peter Owen. She may quite simply have had enough of hospital visits, of compulsory attendance at drug management units and of the whole ennui of human existence. She had once reminded Raymond Marriott that 'depression is as good an introduction to oblivion as any other'. Her existential fortitude had her accept depression as a generic substrate to living – a largely endemic state that she attempted to alter chemically or by using her art as a tool to reinvent reality. Both worked to a degree as temporary palliatives for a permanent condition. This is not to say that she was generally morose or depressed in company or that she was pathologically different on her last day. Did she in fact inject herself more than once and die in the process? The fact that she died with a loaded syringe in her hand does not mean that she had not injected herself previously. Mismanagement and accidents are a common cause of death among intravenous addicts, and Anna may simply have miscalculated.

The funeral took place at Golders Green Crematorium on a cold blue mid-December day in 1968. It was attended by Rhys Davies, Raymond Marriott, Rose Knox-Peebles, Diana Johns, Peter Owen and Theophilia Bluth. 'How cold, how unaffectionate she was,' Mrs Bluth pronounced with malice to a shocked Rose Knox-Peebles in the car back from the crematorium, as they made their way to a small gathering, with sherry and smoked salmon sandwiches at Hillsleigh Road.

Private to the end, Anna requested that her ashes be buried in her garden, beneath a laurel tree.

Postscript
Where Are You Now?

*

Jean Cocteau once remarked that poets never really die, they only pretend to. If the work has staying power it lives on independently of its author, unreconstructed and fixed by the limitations of the time in which it was conceived. We read a book and date it by its terminology, in the same way as we identify a pop song by the decade in which it was produced. The artist is indissolubly linked not only to his or her neurobiology but to the knowledge available at that time. If molecular biology succeeded in preventing the body's cells from dying – perhaps by protecting the DNA so that cells could continue dividing indefinitely – then the literature and art founded on the crisis of mortality would be rendered obsolete. Writing pushes the moment to its parameters and stops there. The visionary succeeds in going beyond those barriers.

Like all dead authors Anna Kavan can neither revise nor add to the work she has written, and yet the reinvention continues. I find myself in the process of writing this book representing her in the present, talking about her to friends and aficionados as if she were alive, and on a recent visit to Hillsleigh Road I actually caught sight of a thin, blonde woman in a pastel jumper and slacks, secateurs in hand, Gucci dark glasses rucked in her hair, standing on her roof terrace. I tell myself it is a trick of the light. There was a mimosa in flower that day, almost opposite Anna's house, its yellow flowers explosive with scent, despite the abrasive February cold.

One of the liveliest of Anna's recent critics, Elizabeth Young, is worth quoting for the fizz she brings to her perceptions. Using her review of David Callard's biography as the occasion for an extended essay on drug-related literature in a piece collected in *Pandora's Handbag*, she writes with profound empathy for Kavan the addict. She is not entirely in agreement with those of Anna's friends who seek to normalize her image, as though by drawing attention to her elegance and hard work they are denying the ruthlessness of her addiction.

Such attempts to distance Kavan from her drug, although well meaning, are misleading. She was one of those rare writers who did not publish at all until she was habituated. Heroin was the centre of her existence; it was her lover, her religion, her salvation, and almost all of her later work charts the process of addiction in an extraordinary pure and crystalline form using again and again images – of cold, of ice, of forbidding landscapes, lowering castles and forbidding watchers – in a manner that should be familiar to us from any study of the great addict writers of the Romantic period.

If you are sufficiently courageous to commit to your art and not worry about money, others take care of you. The commissions help. Anna got by with and without money, and Young rightly argues, 'in that Kavan had lifelong access to clean legal drugs, there was no reason at all why she should not appear cheerful, well-groomed, hard working and so on. It is not the narcotics themselves that cause indigence, dishevelment and disease but the laws that criminalize the addict.'

I would argue that normal people do not create imaginative art. The compensation, the feeling of uniqueness that is part of the creative experience, and the need to continuously re-vision reality, are not the psychological quotient required by most people to get by. For Anna Kavan writing was a way of dialoguing her fears and looking at them like cells in a culture dish. She knew ultimately that writing makes nothing happen except inside the mind. Its self-limitations extend to no one other than a few serious readers. A lot of a writer's time is spent wondering why nobody reads.

There are too many unnecessary books in the world. The culture is saturated. Walking into chain stores such as Borders and Waterstone's is like entering a meat-rack of hyped titles, the stacks on the tables waiting to be thumbed before joining the list of publishers' returns. If the author does not network or promote a book, it is as good as dead. Unless they are in the know, how does anyone differentiate the good from the bad? How do you find Anna Kavan?

She is there somewhere as a survivalist at a time of urban apocalypse. There is something in the London air that her paranoia radar picked up on a long time ago – London as the epicentre of the end of things. The slide into lawlessness, homicide, authoritarian politicians conveyed across the city in armour-plated Jaguars, a Prime Minister in a bulletproof vest pacing his bunker in the corridors under Whitehall, his index of war crimes hanging over the city like a radioactive halo: this is an update of the Kavan register, a reincarnation of the anonymous sadists who stalk the pages of her fiction. This is the digital, dehumanized city that Anna Kavan anticipated. London's commissar, with his appointed 'tsars' as ministers, is not so far removed from the brutally corrupt warden in *Ice* who is always accompanied by his bodyguard. 'He usually jumped straight into his big car and was driven off at tremendous speed.' Anna's prescient sense of impending global catastrophe permeated her fiction at a time when only science-fiction writers brokered flame-out landscapes. In *Ice* she wrote herself into the future, which is our present.

> There was talk of a secret act of aggression by some foreign power, but no one knew what had actually happened. The government would not disclose the facts. I was informed privately of a steep rise in radioactive pollution, pointing to the explosion of a nuclear device, but of an unknown type, the consequences of which could not be accurately predicted. It was possible that polar modifications had resulted, and would lead to a substantial climatic change due to the refraction of solar heat. If the melting antarctic ice cap flowed over the South Pacific and Atlantic oceans, a vast ice-mass would be created, reflecting the sun's rays and throwing them back into outer space, thus depriving the earth of warmth. In town, everything was chaotic and contradictory. News from abroad was censored, but travel was left unrestricted. Confusion was increased by a spate of new and conflicting regulations, and by the arbitrary way controls were imposed or lifted.

Good writing imagines its future rather than looks back at its historicized past. It is easy to work with history because the facts are there to be massaged and reordered. The future is always the writer's present, and it is a risk to use what is around now in its immediate state and reconfigure it as part of continuity. This of course is the function of the visionary, or the one who is intrepid enough to pursue that experiential highway. On a neurochemical level we can argue that it all takes place in the wiring of the amygdala, an almond-shaped complex of interconnected structures buried in the depths of the temporal lobe next to the hippocampus. The amygdala governs emotions, and in types like Anna it is the black box recorder of fear. A genetic predisposition or trauma may lead to an over-large amygdala, and hyperactivity in its functioning may damage the hippocampus, affecting its ability to regulate powerful stress hormones, which can also harm other regions of the brain. It has been suggested that depression, far from being a simple matter of depleted neurotransmitters, may actually have its origins in raised cortisol levels that lead to shrinkage of the hippocampus and the enlargement of the amygdala. This may explain in part the shared acutely visual vocabulary of images that such writers utilize. It is not that a disregulated amygdala promotes the work but rather the psychological components of imagination are finer tuned to this neurologically disordered modem.

According to Elizabeth Young,

> Kavan's life has many parallels with that of Jean Rhys. Both were terribly damaged in infancy; both grew up gifted, suspicious and alienated. Both were addicts – Rhys was an alcoholic. Both at times referred to the hostile outer world of authority and bureaucracy as 'the Machine'. Neither made money from their fiction and both suffered long periods of obscurity from which they were rescued by kind and perspicacious publishers. Both achieved fame posthumously. Carole Angier, Rhys's biographer, tells us that Rhys suffered from 'borderline personality disorder', features of which are addiction, isolation and paranoia. For what it's worth, this diagnosis must also apply to Kavan.

Diagnosis apart, the analogy is a useful one, for not only did the two writers admire each other's work, but each wrote for themselves first and the reader second. A popular novelist harnessed to a large advance has little option but to tailor the work to a potential readership if she or he is to earn from the book. Kavan, like Rhys, had no such expectation. Their job was writing out of a psychic organization and without the incentive of money. They wrote for no one and changed the world by what they discovered in themselves along the way. According to David Callard's computations, Anna's entire literary earnings for the 1950s were under £100 – her advances from Peter Owen on *Eagle's Nest* and *A Bright Green Field* amounting to £25 each. The rest came from occasional stories published in magazines. The reward was in the writing, not in payment for the work done. Anna existed largely on the £600-a-year allowance paid her by her stepfather Hugh Tevis. The idea that she was comfortable is unfounded, and the precariousness of her existence contributed greatly to her anxiety.

According to Raymond Marriott, 'She cast doubts, she lied, she fabricated, she spoke the truth, she was not honest. Where did it begin and where did it end?' The answer of course is that it does not. Anna's duplicities were not just the programmatic data of the drug, they were the contradictory behaviour of a survivalist committed to her art.

As with Anaïs Nin, the lies and manipulations were directed solely towards protecting the work. Nobody pays for the time needed to write unpopular books, and the resultant insecurity on the writer's part may trigger patterns of scheming conditioned by the need to survive. Whatever money came to Anna she invested in writing. Hugh Tevis had little conception of her real stature as a writer, but his allowance kept her on the page.

In recent years Anna Kavan's work has graduated into Peter Owen's prestigious Modern Classics series, the small gold pocket books taking her work out into the world again in a new, affordable format. Their availability at least ensures that her books continue to infiltrate stores and are there for the finding. Jenny Sturm is busy writing a dissertation about Anna Kavan's time in New Zealand, and other potential biographers continue to sniff at her trail.

For Brian Aldiss *Ice* remains Kavan's imperishable diamond of a novel, as he explained in *Trillion Year Spree*.

Some of *Ice*'s illustrious relations are clear: Kafka for a start. Anna Kavan's assumed name began with a K in his honour. There is also a surrealist vein, as exhibited in some of Cocteau's work and in the painter De Chirico's only novel *Hebdomeros*. Again, *Ice* is a catastrophe work that goes as far beyond Ballard as Ballard is beyond Wyndham, sailing into the chilly air of metaphysics. It looks sideways at its great contemporary among pornographic novels, Pauline Réage's *Story of O*. Even more, it is its own self, mysterious, in some ways unsatisfactory, an enigma – like all the greatest science fiction, approaching despair, but, in its acceptance of the insoluble, also full of a blind force much like hope.

You cannot write without hope being somewhere in the mix. Hope was in the internal sunlight that Anna chased as part of her vision. It was also in the portentous, hypnotic landscapes of *Eagle's Nest*, *Who Are You?*, *The Parson* and *Ice*, all of which are distinguished by a sensual imagery that transforms their redoubtable wasteland topologies into precincts characterized by the beautiful but indifferent proliferation of nature.

193

What did Anna Kavan do on bad days? Write a letter to Raymond Marriott downstairs, make a cup of Harrods Blend 49 tea, sit outside in the ecosphere of her Kensington garden, pick at a box of chocolates and wonder why and how it had all begun to go wrong; but ultimately also hope. The resolve was written into her, which is why on an instinctual level her body fought successfully against carefully administered overdoses so often. If her existential overview of humanity was essentially nihilistic, then the lyricism of her writing lifts it above the dysphoria she felt about life. The conversion happened naturally in the process of writing, as though words reset the homeostasis of her mood, having her communicate a despair coloured by the realization that negativity could be made habitable by poetry. This was her art, and the affirmation of hope happened involuntarily.

But there was an end in the hard fact of her death. Elizabeth Young writes of how 'It is intolerably sad to contemplate this elderly and distinguished writer suffering the indignities of a clinic and the brusque attention of a doctor, insensible of Kavan's gifts, who thought of addicts in terms of stereotypes.' This was the dilemma that arguably made death acceptable for her in her last years, and I still incline towards the notion of her suicide. Dr Oppenheim at the Charing Cross Hospital addiction clinic was not in sympathy with creativity or modified habits aimed at suppressing anxiety as the subtext to addiction. Perhaps Oppenheim, with her governmentally enforced policy, was referring to Anna as one of her failures when in the context of the interview I have quoted, she said, 'Currently we have only two patients left who are on heroin only. And they are chaotic.' Anna had no intention of functioning in the community and should not have been in that clinic. Methadone would have subdued her into inactivity, and a woman of her age and superior intelligence had little to learn from Dr Oppenheim's equation of drugs with socially dysfunctional behaviour.

I am writing the last pages of this book on a blowy May evening sitting on the pavement opposite Anna's old house in Hillsleigh Road. She maintained that 'heroin had saved my life and kept me from madness'. Today the average London adult has a cocktail of chemicals in his or her body including organochlorine pesticides, phthalates, brominated flame retardants, PCBs from electronic components and prefluorinated compounds. We are full of DDT and industrial chemicals. Anna was, too, but to a lesser degree. Heroin was her chemical, and she stayed with it to the end.

There is a huge chestnut tree unscrolling white flowers at the foot of Hillsleigh Road on the Holland Park Avenue side. The cars burning up the narrow road are the Grand Cherokees and Range Rovers driven by paramilitary professionals, with blacked-out windows as though in preparation for the urban conflagration that Kavan knew would happen one day. Bangs of blue wistaria swoop over the wall of her old garden in tumbling dreadlocks; but most noticeable, and probably an outtake from the garden she cultivated, are the perfectly coloured off-white roses with a hint of pink at the centre that project over the wall parallel with the wistaria. A sign from Anna? They are certainly her colour, and despite the unseasonable cold they point resolutely to the beginnings of summer.

Bibliography of Anna Kavan's works

*

HELEN FERGUSON

A Charmed Circle. London: Jonathan Cape, 1929

The Dark Sisters. London: Jonathan Cape, 1930

Let Me Alone. London: Jonathan Cape, 1930

A Stranger Still. London. John Lane, 1935

Goose Cross. London: John Lane, 1936

Rich Get Rich. London: John Lane, 1937

ANNA KAVAN

Asylum Piece and Other Stories. London: Jonathan Cape, 1940

Change the Name. London: Jonathan Cape, 1941

I Am Lazarus: Short Stories. London: Jonathan Cape, 1945

Sleep Has His House. London: Cassell, 1948

The Horse's Tale (with K.T. Bluth). London: Gaberbocchus Press, 1949

A Scarcity of Love. Southport, Lancashire: Angus Downie, 1956

Eagles' Nest. London: Peter Owen, 1957

A Bright Green Field. London: Peter Owen, 1958

Who Are You? Lowestoft, Suffolk: Scorpion Press, 1963

Ice. London: Peter Owen, 1967

Julia and the Bazooka and Other Stories. London: Peter Owen, 1970

My Soul in China: A Novella and Stories. London: Peter Owen, 1975

My Madness: The Selected Writings of Anna Kavan (edited with an
introduction by Brian Aldiss). London: Picador, 1990

Mercury. London: Peter Owen, 1994

The Parson. London: Peter Owen, 1995

Books Consulted

*

I WOULD LIKE TO thank the McFarlin Library at the University of Tulsa for permission to quote from 'The Cactus Sign', an unpublished manuscript of Anna Kavan's housed in their collection of her papers, as well as from writings, letters and documents of hers in their possession. My thanks, too, go to Lewis Davies and the National Library of Wales for permission to use extracts from Anna Kavan's correspondence with Rhys Davies.

Aldiss, Brian W., *Trillion Year Spree* (with David Wingrove). London: Gollancz, 1986

Bentall, Richard P., *Madness Explained: Psychosis and Human Nature*. London, Allen Lane, 2003

Burkhart, Charles, *Herman and Nancy and Ivy: Three Lives in Art*. London: Gollancz, 1977

Callard, David, *The Case of Anna Kavan*. London: Peter Owen, 1992

Gascoyne, David, *The Sun at Midnight*. London: Enitharmon Press, 1970

—, *Journal 1936–37*. London: Enitharmon Press, 1980

—, *Paris Journal 1937–39*. London: Enitharmon Press, 1978

Green, Jonathon, *All Dressed Up: The Sixties and the Counterculture*. London: Jonathan Cape, 1998

Hewitt, Paolo, *The Sharper Word: A Mod Anthology*. London: Helter Skelter Publishing, 1999

Isherwood, Christopher, *Lost Years: A Memoir 1945–51* (edited and introduced by Katherine Bucknell). London. Chatto and Windus, 2000

Laing, Adrian, *R.D. Laing: A Biography*. London: Peter Owen, 1994

Laing, R.D., *The Divided Self*. London: Tavistock, 1960

—, *Self and Others*. London: Tavistock, 1961

Levy, Shawn, *Ready, Steady, Go! Swinging London and the Invention of Cool.*
London: Fourth Estate, 2002
Lewis, Jeremy, *Cyril Connolly: A Life.* London: Jonathan Cape, 1997
Nin, Anaïs, *The Novel of the Future.* London: Peter Owen, 1969
Plant, Sadie, *Writings on Drugs.* London: Faber and Faber, 1999
Shorter, Edward, *A History of Psychiatry from the Era of the Asylum to the Age of Prozac.* London: John Wiley, 1997
Young, Elizabeth, *Pandora's Handbag.* London: Serpent's Tail, 2001

I have in addition relied greatly on biographical details of Anna Kavan's later life supplied as a private typescript by Rose Knox-Peebles, without whom little of Anna's life at Hillsleigh Road would be known. I am indebted to her for her finely tuned attention to detail and to information given me in interviews with her, Peter Owen, Francis King and Bruce Hunter.

May Anna's torch burn brightly.

Index

*

Unless otherwise indicated, all books and stories are by Anna Kavan

My Soul in China 29–30, 31–2, 34, 35, 36, 48, 54, 55, 65, 67, 78, 141, 179

Nadja (André Breton) 149
Naked Lunch, The (William Burroughs) 153
Nelson, Michael 89, 91
Neumann, Robert 92
New Statesman 42, 103
New Writing 103
New Yorker 97, 131
'New Zealand: Answer to an Inquiry' 64
Nin, Anaïs 34, 51, 132, 139, 154–5, 177, 193
Nottingham Central Hospital 82, 107
Nova 173, 174
Novalis (Friedrich von Hardenberg) 95, 97, 107, 108
Novel of the Future, The (Anaïs Nin) 155
'Now and Then' 32

'Old Address, The' 162
'One of the Hot Spots' 58
Oppenheim, Gisella Brigitte 118–19, 174, 194
Orwell, George 51, 91, 110
Osborne, John 123
'Oswald and Rejane' 149
Owen, Peter 45, 128, 132, 136–7, 138, 139, 145, 146, 150, 154–5, 161, 166, 173, 174, 176, 177, 179, 182, 184, 187, 192, 193
Oxford Companion to English Literature 182

Pandora's Handbag (Elizabeth Young) 189
Parkinson, Sir John 82
Parson, The 150, 180, 187, 193
Parson Mead School (Ashtead, Surrey) 16
Paul of Greece, Prince 90
Payne, John 128, 129
Payne, Susan 128
Penrose, Roland 50
Peter Jones (department store) 157
Picador 174, 179
Picasso, Pablo 90
Pink Floyd 154

Plath, Sylvia 106, 139, 146, 179, 181
Plato 97
Plotinus 97
Poe, Edgar Allan 116, 125
Poliuto (Gaetano Donizetti) 155
Pollen (Novalis) 108
Porown, Mr 68
Powell, Anthony 149
Powys, John Cooper 44
Presley, Elvis 181
Pretty Things 138
Proust, Marcel 142, 155
Punch 40

Quadrant Press 176

Rawlings, John 109
Réage, Pauline 144, 193
Rebel Without a Cause 116
Reed, Lou 6, 115, 169
'Revival of Schelling, The' (Karl Theodor Bluth) 140
Rhys, Jean 51, 139, 149, 174, 192
Rich Get Rich 37, 44–5
Richards, Keith 122, 135
Riley, Bridget 154
Robbe-Grillet, Alain 102, 130, 149
Robert Fraser Gallery 154
'Rock Around the Clock' (Bill Haley and His Comets) 116
Rodez asylum 160
Rolling Stones 135, 138
Rommel, Field Marshal Erwin 69
Room in Chelsea Square, A (Michael Nelson) 91
Rousseau, Henri 172
Royal Marsden Hospital (London) 175

St Charles Hospital 175
St George's Church 136
St Mary's Hospital 115
St Peter's Church (Berkshire) 19
St Stephen's Hospital (London) 81, 82
Salisbury (pub) 155, 162
Sally Can't Dance (Lou Reed) 169
Salmon, Andrew 124

Watson, Peter 89, 90–1, 92, 93, 98, 107, 161, 184
'We Know All the Answers', 54
Weekend Telegraph 159, 181
Weidenfeld and Nicolson 139
Welch, Denton 92, 172
Wertheim Gallery 31
Whistler, James McNeill 100
White House, London 100, 103
Who, The 138, 143
Who Are You? 19, 20, 132, 149, 150–6, 193
Wide Sargasso Sea, The (Jean Rhys) 149
Wild One, The 116
Wilde, Oscar 186–7
Williams, Bill 83
Windmill, The 94–5
Winterson, Jeanette 139–40
Witherby, Anthony 90

Witherby, H. and F. 90
Wolfskehl, Karl 64
Woods, Annie Sybella (great-grandmother) 159
Woods, Claude Charles Edward (father) 15, 16
Woods, Helen (mother) *see* Helen Tevis
Woolf, Leonard 175
Woolf, Virginia 51, 91, 92, 93, 139, 175
'Words of Mercury Are Harsh After the Songs of Apollo, The' 149
Wyatt, Woodrow 94
Wyndham, John 193

'Yellow Submarine' (Beatles) 185
Young, Elizabeth 189–90, 192, 194

'Zebra-struck, The' 84, 85–6, 87, 120

THE WORKS OF ANNA KAVAN

Asylum Piece

A Bright Green Field (stories)

Change the Name

A Charmed Circle

Eagles' Nest

I Am Lazarus (stories)

Ice

Julia and the Bazooka (stories)

Let Me Alone

Mercury

My Soul in China (novella and stories)

A Scarcity of Love

Sleep Has His House

A Stranger Still

Who Are You?

FORTHCOMING:

Guilty a recently discovered, previously unpublished novel

20894985R00129

Printed in Great Britain
by Amazon